fr 2.50

Bonsai

Christine Stewart

Bonsai

ORBIS · LONDON

Half title page — *Flowering japonica (ornamental quince) in the cascade style.*
Title page — *A 250-year-old Chinese juniper, a rare specimen bonsai.*
This page — *Informal upright mountain maple in spectacular autumn foliage.*

© 1981 by Orbis Publishing Limited. First published in Great Britain by Orbis Publishing Limited, London 1981

Reprinted 1986 by Orbis Book Publishing Corporation Ltd. A BPCC plc company

Printed in Czechoslovakia
ISBN 0-85613-066-4
50147/3

Contents

The Art of Bonsai

Bonsai, despite their exotic connotations, are simply miniature trees raised in small pots. Not to be confused with genetically dwarfed varieties of tree which remain the same size without any help from the grower, bonsai are tiny replicas of their full-grown brethren in forest and garden, formed over the years by man's patience and skill. Contrary to general belief, no esoteric techniques are employed in bonsai culture. Despite their far-flung ancestry — bonsai is the Japanese word for a plant in a pot — and many misconceptions, the little trees are created not by savagery or starvation but by everyday gardening methods such as pruning and potting.

Yet a faithful small-scale reproduction of any tree will not necessarily capture the spirit of bonsai, which is to encapsulate, in a container, a memorable aspect of nature. Bonsai are, in fact, stylized forms of trees in the wild, the relationship of the miniature to its shallow container playing an integral part in creating the overall impression of unity. And, to be worthy of the name, good bonsai should combine the effects of trunk, branches, leaves, flowers and fruit in a totally harmonious whole. A dwarfed juniper with twisted trunk and shapely branch structure, a tiny azalea in full bloom, a maple bonsai covered in the multi-coloured leaves of autumn, all convey the beauty of wild trees in their natural environment in a condensed and spectacular form.

Age in bonsai is no prerequisite of quality. Neither is cost nor the extent of miniaturization. Measured from the base of the trunk to the tip, bonsai range from the tiny trees known as *mame bonsai* — up to 15 centimetres (6 inches) high — to the really tall ones which can grow to a height of over 90 centimetres (3 feet). The latter will take many years to achieve true beauty but a mame bonsai may be delightful within three years, and a fast-growing medium-sized tree of about 50 centimetres (20 inches) should make a very acceptable bonsai after eight to ten years' training.

Indeed, one of the joys of bonsai is that they can be grown from seed or taken from the wild

Informal upright pyracantha in colourful autumn berry. A popular bonsai tree, the 'firethorn', as it is commonly known, differs from its relative, the cotoneaster in that it has thorny branches. Photographed in May, this particular tree is unusual as it was bearing fruit formed the previous September.

by relatively inexperienced beginners. Certainly, reserves of patience will be called upon while the seedlings mature, but the enthusiast can start work immediately on a wild tree, achieving noticeable results in a comparatively short period.

Nor should a bonsai which is undistinguished as an individual tree be dismissed out of hand. A lone pine of indifferent shape, for instance, can take on new meaning if grouped with others on a shallow tray or arranged to form part of a scene in a miniature garden. These gardens, unlike the deep tub and sink versions, offer interest in their skilful use of perspective combined with an overall simplicity of design. By carefully positioning a conifer, say, or a windswept style of tree in relation to attractive rocks, sand and moss, a whole scene can be recaptured in a limited space. Similarly, a number of saplings planted in forest-like profusion on a large oval tray can be very effective, masking the immaturity that would be obvious in individual bonsai and recreating a much-loved landscape.

Newcomers to bonsai, who fear their lack of artistic talent, should not be deterred by the emphasis placed on aesthetic appreciation; a well-developed sense of design should be considered a bonus but is not essential. Flower-arrangers, for instance, may more easily comprehend the basic relationships of shapes, proportions and colours of bonsai, but everyone can learn from looking at established trees in city parks and squares as well as in the open countryside. It is no exaggeration to say that working with bonsai offers something to everyone, from those who enjoy any aspect of gardening to those with the highest artistic aspirations.

There are problems, of course, but these are usually due to lack of experience. Because bonsai are small they are commonly mistaken for indoor plants. In fact, they should simply remain in whatever conditions are natural to growth. Tropical bonsai, therefore, which would obviously flourish in tropical climates, might well, like houseplants, grow well indoors. The majority of bonsai, however, are accustomed to growing outside in temperate weather and are quite happy exposed to the elements in the garden or on the patio. Evergreen bonsai go through a semi-dormant period and deciduous species drop their leaves in the autumn—facts frequently not appreciated by tender-hearted owners who rush the trees inside at the first sign of a cold snap, often to a centrally-heated death.

A pyracantha in full bloom in the early summer. This shrub is noted for its spectacular blossom, similar to that of the hawthorn. The varying display throughout the seasons makes the pyracantha an excellent subject for bonsai, especially as it is quick-growing, hardy and happy in most fertile soils.

Similarly, over-watering or excessive feeding can be equally destructive and errors of pruning may take years to correct.

Such initial problems are more than offset by the lasting pleasure to be derived from bonsai. Enthusiasm for the dwarfed trees is frequently accompanied by a widening knowledge of trees in general, so that even those in urban environments take on greater significance. An increased awareness of other aspects of the countryside often results too. Above all, cultivating miniature trees is a calming activity which, apart from the intrinsic satisfaction of growing bonsai at home, provides an added therapeutic and relaxing bonus. The shape of the trees, the texture of the bark, the colour and scents of the flowers and foliage, all speak for themselves in what can only be referred to as a living, constantly changing work of art.

Are there no snags, then? Very few, apart from those encountered in the ordinary horticultural practices of potting and pruning, feeding and watering and so on. But be warned, growing bonsai is not for those unprepared to devote just a few minutes a day to their hobby. High standards of health and care are needed, along with an enquiring mind in working out what is best for certain trees. In short, be prepared to combine strong self-discipline with a practical streak and an unfettered imagination.

An ability to compromise is perhaps even more essential. A bonsai can sometimes offer scope far beyond that suggested by initial impressions, so be prepared to 'file away' a new tree for a few months until new growth may suggest other possibilities. Learn as much as possible from books and experts, but always keep an open mind. The very best bonsai are beautiful in their own right, not necessarily because they observe set forms. Respect the disciplines of the Japanese masters, but do not be limited by hard and fast rules supposedly laid down by them. Bear these precepts in mind at all times to gain great satisfaction and enrichment from a comparatively simple and not necessarily expensive hobby.

The Bonsai Tradition

For over a thousand years Japan has been acknowledged as the home of bonsai. During that time the Japanese have brought the art of dwarfing trees to perfection; they created the basic bonsai styles, established the principles and drew up the terminology. That they did not originate the idea, however, is shown by ancient Chinese paintings from the Sung Dynasty (AD 960–1280) which depict naturally dwarfed trees in containers, serving an ornamental function in room settings. Nature's own bonsai, formed by harsh winds and poor positions, they were presumably taken straight from the wild and potted.

Trade with Japan resulted in the practice being assimilated by that industrious nation, where collecting trees became a rich man's craze, with teams of carriers travelling vast distances in search of distinctive specimens. There are references to bonsai in the records of the Kasuga shrine in the Kamakura period (1192–1333) and the little trees are also shown on scrolls of the same period.

Though we have little knowledge of the state of bonsai in mainland China today, trees in Hong Kong and Taiwan reflect the Republic's thinking. Chinese bonsai are noticeably different from Japanese, being trained, as far as we know, almost entirely by pruning, with very little use of

This large, six-panel folding screen was painted in the Edo period in Japan, during the first half of the eighteenth century, by Bunkaku. It depicts a popular form of entertainment at this time, a puppet show, rather like the English ballad drama in which the narrative was sung to music. The puppets were apparently so sophisticated that the audience quite forgot the operators who were in full view of them. This particular play, The Story of the Potted Dwarf Trees, performed here by the Takemoto Theatre of Osaka, is of especial interest to bonsai enthusiasts, as it demonstrates the great value of the little trees. Set in the political tumult of the thirteenth century, it tells of a Buddhist priest seeking shelter at the house of an exiled warrior. The visitor is at first refused entry as the family fear that they do not have enough provisions for him. Finally, thoughts of the priest outside in the snow cause the woman of the house to invite him in. During the bitterly cold night the three bonsai pictured on the left of the screen had to be sacrificed for fuel. The warrior's hospitality was rewarded, however, when the priest, who was in reality a high official, returned home and, to thank the family, awarded them three large estates, one for each of the precious bonsai.

wire. Bonsai styles appear to vary from north to south and perhaps more detailed knowledge of Chinese methods of training and cultivation may spring from the country's present open-door policy.

While China is characteristically reticent about her trees, Japan has developed bonsai growing into a major industry with a vast home market and jealous export controls. This is small wonder when one looks at Japanese technology, as reflected by the electronics industry, which shows the same ability to copy, improve and miniaturize. Such 'mass production' of bonsai has unfortunately led to a decline in standards, and some of the many trees imported from Japan are scarred and over-wired. The concern with growth rather than quality is a reflection of

economic life in Japan where the increasing pressures of industrial society encourage workers to leave the countryside to seek a higher standard of living in the towns and cities. Old people, left behind, retain their traditional bonsai skills but there are few young people willing to be taught. Nevertheless, many good Japanese trees are still exported, though their rigid adherence to form may make them appear somewhat unbalanced to the Western eye.

Serious bonsai creation is, however, being practised with increasing flair and dedication outside Japan. For a period after World War II, when most Japanese things tended to be shunned, Western bonsai practitioners became too inward-looking, producing trees acceptable only to themselves. This lack of reverence for tradi-

Facing page: Japanese bonsai nurseries are almost works of art. The Western grower is overwhelmed by the abundance of trees and the quiet beauty of the setting. Note how the trees, some of them quite large, are displayed on staging.

Above: Detail from a thirteenth-century Japanese scroll of the Kamakura period, depicting the life of the priest Kobo who visited T'ang China to study Esoteric Buddhist doctrines. Here he is receiving secret teachings, transmitted only orally by the ancients. Note the bonsai on the balcony, an interesting reminder that the little trees were already established in Japan at this early date and a reference to their Chinese origins.

Below: Detail of a Chinese handscroll by Lu-Chi, painted at the time of the Ming dynasty, c. 1554. This landscape, of the autumn colours at Hsün-Yang, with its stunted, twisted trees, is indicative of the type of terrain from which the original bonsai were taken and trained.

tion was particularly apparent in Britain but was not so marked in the United States where the guidance of generations of Japanese immigrants played a major part in ensuring the development of good bonsai.

Despite a more open attitude and a desire to learn, radical differences still exist between Japanese and Western bonsai. Perhaps the cultural divide is just too great ever to be entirely bridged. The rigid observance by the Japanese of many traditions, such as the tea ceremony and ikebana (classical oriental flower-arranging), reflects a formalized background in which every aspect of life is given due weight and meaning. Ikebana has much in common with bonsai cultivation: the emphasis is always on line and shape rather than colour and density. Certain numbers and angles of flowers have religious symbolic value and the length of line is related to emotion and the outline shape frequently encompasses a whole scene. The art of classic bonsai contains representations of the sun, moon and mother figure, as well as the heavens and the earth. With the best will in the world, it is virtually impossible for most Western minds to comprehend such thinking.

The chasm of spiritual understanding is not made any narrower by the contrast in physical environment. Surrounded, outside the density of major cities, by a countryside landscaped in many instances to achieve a cultivated ideal of beauty and by a day-to-day existence in which mountains and rivers are reflected in all aspects of design, there is little wonder that the average

Previous page: The 400-year-old garden of the New Otani Hotel, Tokyo, Japan. Only four real gardens exist in the world's most populous city where land is at such a premium that a law limits the amount of space each householder is allowed, regardless of income. Little wonder that the inhabitants cultivate bonsai on patios and terraces. Existing gardens are protected by law, however, and pine trees — symbols of longevity in Ikebana — cannot be destroyed, so that very aged, ailing specimens are propped up, as they are in this garden.

Right: Though idealized, this detail from a mid-sixteenth-century screen painting by Sesson, showing the seasons of autumn and winter, gives an idea of the type of Japanese countryside still existing outside the major cities, where mountains, streams and trees are part of most people's daily life.

inhabitant of, say, Osaka will probably see far more potential in a jagged old tree than his counterpart in Liverpool or Des Moines. It is no coincidence that every Japanese child spends a great deal of early school life practising an art such as calligraphy. By adopting free expression in all things at the expense of self-limitation and technique, the West may well be the artistic loser.

It is all too easy, then, to see why there are such differences between the native bonsai of Japan and those of other countries — which is not necessarily to condemn Western bonsai, the best of which have a charm of their own. Japanese bonsai are divided into specimen, semi-specimen and commercial trees. True specimen trees — aged bonsai of outstanding classical shape maintained at the peak of form — are comparatively rare outside Japan; the juniper illustrated at the end of this chapter is one of only a dozen such trees in Britain. More common are the semi-specimen bonsai, already established trees with further potential needing only time and work to create superb bonsai.

Of the thirty or more Japanese bonsai styles, we have depicted ten that are frequently seen in the West. Most of the commonly available European and American trees will adapt happily to training into one or more of these shapes. While the formal upright shape produces a very artificial but perfect tree — an absolutely straight, tapering trunk with a stated sequence of branches — and is usually most successful on needled evergreens, the informal upright — alternate branches with balanced curves coming off a reasonably straight trunk — is a more natural shape, suiting most deciduous species.

Equally popular for both deciduous and evergreen bonsai is the pine style with its curving trunk and layered horizontal branches. Also with a natural look, though in fact usually the result of very skilled training, is the windswept style with all its branches generally streaming in one direction only. Many bad examples of this style exist and it is not sufficient to try to overcome the defects of a 'problem' tree simply by potting it at an angle as is often done. The novice should be cautious of the apparent simplicity of the broom style which is primarily seen in zelkova elms. The bush-like head with its fine, upward-growing structure of twigs and branches takes many years to achieve.

Driftwood-style bonsai are generally aged, needled evergreens, the magnificent deadwood being the result of many years' growing in the

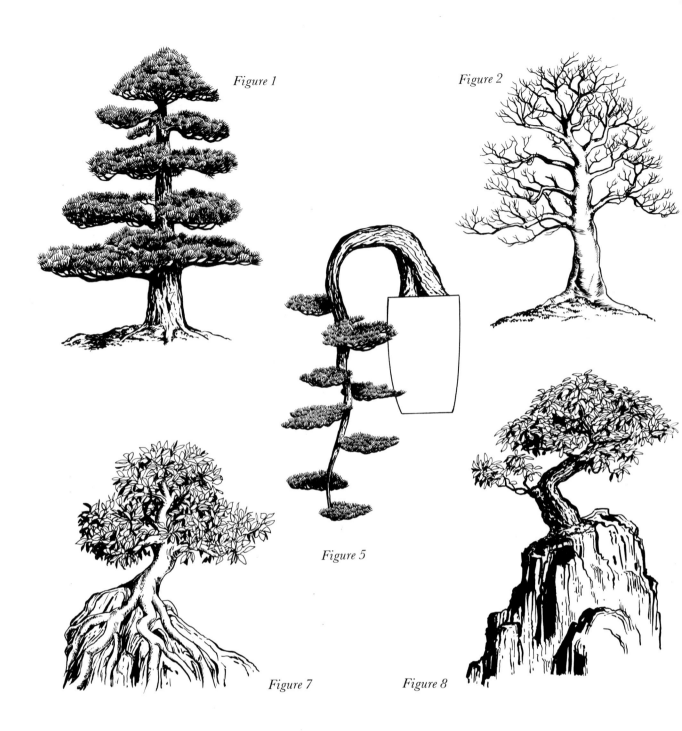

Figure 1

Figure 2

Figure 5

Figure 7

Figure 8

Figure 1 Formal Upright The most regular of all the bonsai shapes, the formal upright comprises a very straight single trunk, gradually tapering to its full height from a firm base. Strong roots radiating around the trunk give an impression of permanence. Perfection of shape is achieved by the branches which alternate on either side of the trunk in a set pattern. The most suitable trees for training in this style are needled evergreens such as pine or Japanese cedar, but such symmetry is very difficult to achieve and should not be attempted by beginners.

Figure 2 Informal Upright This variation on the formal upright also features a straight trunk and alternate branches, but the emphasis is more on a good natural outline than perfect branch arrangement. It is

the most popular bonsai style as it is fairly simple for even newcomers to the art of bonsai, and suits most easily available deciduous species such as beech, maple, oak, hornbeam etc.

Figure 3 Driftwood Also referred to as the coiled style, the most prominent feature of this impressive bonsai shape is the single curved and twisted trunk with its harsh bark and lots of dead wood. Most successful driftwood bonsai are aged evergreens such as pine and juniper taken from harsh conditions in the wild and trained. The impression of age can be heightened by bleaching the dead wood, and a similar effect is achieved on young, sinuous trees, by stripping off the bark with a special jinning tool, although, again, this work is for experienced hands only.

Figure 3

Figure 4

Figure 6

Figure 9

Figure 10

Figure 4 Windswept Another style denoting a harsh environment, the windswept bonsai always grows at a pronounced angle. The trunk leans to right or left and all the branches grow in that same direction, as if the tree were growing on a cliff top, constantly blown sideways by strong winds. The best windswept bonsai are trained from those types of small-leaved trees which are usually found in exposed places, such as pine, juniper, cypress, yew etc.

Figure 5 Cascade The basic feature of this style is the leaning trunk with branches hanging over the side of the pot. In a true cascade the branches must fall below the bottom of the container, whereas branches which hang over the rim of the pot but do not reach its base form only a semi-cascade. A deep, narrow container is needed to balance such a style. A multitude of styles can be found under the general cascade umbrella, depending on the basic shape and how it is viewed. For instance, the attractive 'waterfall' comprises several branches weeping from one trunk down the front or side of the container. Shown here is a particularly steep drop with no crown, somewhat extreme and confined mainly to coniferous species.

Figure 6 Raft Although it may take many years to achieve, a good raft bonsai is very satisfying. Briefly, the trunk of the tree chosen to be trained as a raft is potted on its side, with its branches wired to grow upwards, thus forming new trunks. A shapely, curved root is best, and a too-straight original trunk can be wired into place to produce a more sinuous new root.

Both evergreen and deciduous species are suitable as rafts.

Figure 7 Root Over Rock The main impression from this style is of an isolated tree clinging to a rock face, perhaps above a ravine or on an island. It is achieved by positioning a tree with specially trained long roots on a large, rugged rock with suitable indentations to secure the roots. As the roots grow and thicken, they dominate the rock base, becoming bark-like in texture as extensions of the trunk. Many kinds of maple are suited to this style as their roots swell and fuse easily, as do those of beech and juniper.

Figure 8 Root In Rock A variation of the above style in which the rock is used as the container and the roots trained accordingly. Most species lend themselves to rock plantings, depending on the type of setting to be created. A flat rock bed housing a single tree or a group can depict an arid desert or island landscape, for instance, whereas one or more trees in pockets on a tall, jagged rock, appear mountainous and bleak.

Figure 9 Pine Despite its name, this style is most popularly found in deciduous species, although it is obviously equally appropriate for such conifers as pines and junipers. The single trunk is always bent but with an easy, flowing motion, unlike the twisted driftwood style. The branches form alternate layers with a pronounced top.

Figure 10 Groups To form the impression of a copse or a forest, either evergreens or deciduous trees — never mixed, nor mixed species — are planted following certain principles. Group plantings are an excellent way of utilizing immature trees as the overall shape is more important than the quality of the individual trees.

wild in adverse conditions. It is possible to create a deadwood effect on younger trees of suitable shape by 'jinning' (stripping away the bark with a special tool) and treating the wood, but this should be practised cautiously.

Many flowering trees lend themselves to the cascade style where the branches hang below the bottom of the container. Among the accepted variations are the waterfall, with a number of hanging branches, or a single, gently snaking trunk with minimal branching, falling down the front or side of the pot. In contrast to the 'naturally' hanging cascade, the weeping branch style is practised on informal uprights whose branches, weeping naturally, as with the willow, are then further trained.

Group plantings, as demonstrated in Project 5, can utilize immature trees to produce the effect of a spinney, or more mature trees to create forests of various types. While the numbers are more or less immaterial — three or more trees form a group, and if less than ten the total number should be uneven — rules of perspective should be adhered to. Most so-called 'rules' are only guidelines, principles to be respected rather than slavishly followed. The only real rules to follow are those employed in good horticultural practice. No bonsai expert would expect novice bonsai growers to follow set procedures to produce particular styles of trees. Throughout this book principles will be established, gardening techniques explained and ideas presented so that people can develop them to their own individual tastes. With basic knowledge, understanding and confidence, the creation of bonsai acceptable to all but perfectionists is quite possible.

Right: A specimen bonsai of the highest quality, this 250-year-old Chinese juniper with twisted trunk and spectacular deadwood originated in Japan but is now in England.

Collecting Bonsai

Many and varied are the ways of building up a bonsai collection; how to start depends upon the individual's preferences and pocket. Beginners with some ready cash and a desire for established trees would be best served by purchasing a few good examples from a specialist bonsai nursery. Those readers not wanting a ready-made collection could obtain suitable young trees from any local nursery and train them from scratch, while the truly impecunious of pioneering spirit might gain great satisfaction in digging up dwarfed trees from the wild.

Another simple way of accumulating bonsai is to grow the trees from seed which might be picked up on country walks, in city parks or even in the home garden. But this is a slow process: it takes at least two or three years to produce a small tree suitable for bonsai training. Bearing this in mind, it would be advisable to have one or two larger trees as well, to work on and appreciate while the seedlings put on growth. Similarly, growing from cuttings takes time and is best practised alongside other methods of cultivation. More advanced growers can gain new trees by such skills as air layering and grafting, techniques which should not be attempted by the complete novice.

The bonsai enthusiast is likely to combine several methods of obtaining trees. And, while the nervous beginner may lavish hours of care on a single specimen, it is best to acquire two or three different varieties and styles of trees as soon as possible. A lone bonsai, like an only child, may be the object of too much attention. It can be killed by kindness as a result of overwatering or feeding, or given too much corrective care in training. The grower, too, can only benefit from working on several trees, noting the seasonal effects on different species and learning their distinctive growth habits.

If you are lucky enough to be able to buy several bonsai at once, take the trouble to find a genuine bonsai nursery rather than a general one which might only stock bonsai as a side-line. Bonsai specialists have a reputation to uphold in a rather limited circle of suppliers, whereas other nurserymen may inadvertently harm the trees through lack of knowledge, and so you might find yourself with poor specimens.

Layered hornbeam in the informal upright style: about 60 years old, this is an excellent example of a semi-specimen tree which has been well trained over a long period and has the potential to become a bonsai of great merit.

AN INSTANT COLLECTION

Learn a little about bonsai before you make a purchase. This is often best done by simply looking at as many pictures of good trees as possible. As your taste develops, explain what you have in mind to a specialist and be prepared to take his or her advice. Look for fairly young trees, probably about three to four years old, with good potential which should be relatively inexpensive, and make sure that they are in the correct containers (see page 34 for information on containers).

A collection of half-a-dozen such bonsai should provide variety of species and styles. Try to mix coniferous evergreens — needle varieties such as pine and spruce, or those with hard, scale-like foliage — with small-leaved deciduous trees which drop their leaves in winter but present different aspects in all four seasons. Most of the trees are likely to be of the informal upright style, but a fledgling group or a tree on a rock will add interest to any collection.

A good sample collection from a bonsai nursery might comprise, say, a variety of cotoneaster, a type of maple, a crab apple, a zelkova elm or a hornbeam, an evergreen pine or a juniper. The cotoneaster comes in leaf very early, has attractive flowers in spring, colourful autumn leaves, and holds its glorious red berries well into late winter. Maples, too, have very pretty summer and autumn foliage, with the added advantage that they grow very quickly and any scars made by inexperienced hands cover up well. Crab apples are also easy to train and develop striking flowers and fruit, while Chinese elms, though extremely rare since they are now a prohibited export, present an interesting corky bark. Pines and the Chinese juniper are, of course, two of the classic bonsai subjects.

GENERAL NURSERY TREES

Many of the trees that have been mentioned can be obtained untrained (and so are cheaper) from nurseries which supply them for general garden use. When selecting, say, a beech, a larch, or a hornbeam, always go to a centre known for good stock. Choice will be limited to a certain extent by what is on offer, depending on geographical location and demand, so that there may well be several examples of one variety but only one or two of others. Select from a variety with lots of choice, even if it is not quite what you originally had in mind. What to look for in

purchasing a nursery tree, how to deal with it when it first arrives home and initial training are all dealt with in detail in Project 1.

TREES FROM THE WILD

Digging up wild trees may appear to be a cheap and simple way of collecting bonsai, but it is not for the faint-hearted — extracting the chosen tree may be both frustrating and exhausting. It is not simply a matter of going off to a local wood and just taking any old tree. Firstly, digging up any wild plant without permission is inadvisable; you must check with the landowner before making off with any of his stock.

Secondly, not all trees make good bonsai. Old trees, for instance, dislike violent disturbance and may well die if they are moved. And although it is possible to remove large trees, the preparatory process takes several years. The novice should look for a fairly small tree, not more than about 30 centimetres (12 inches) high, and perhaps five years old, with interesting features. It is always worth remembering that species which bear small leaves will make better miniature trees for obvious reasons.

Good potential bonsai are to be found in unlikely places such as the side of a woodland path where they might have been trodden on when very young but have survived in an interesting shape (see the hawthorn in Project 2). Some very stunted trees with much-branched systems are frequently seen in areas where deer, sheep or cattle graze, as the animals nibble the new shoots each year, thus acting as regular pruners. Dwarfed trees are also found in very exposed situations, their growth stunted by the harsh weather, but these should be approached with caution as they can be particularly difficult to remove. Often far older than their size might indicate, such trees may have developed extremely long roots for anchorage and to draw up distant water, so that digging them up is well nigh impossible. The beginner, then, would do best to collect trees from heath-land, pasture and forest and leave those from mountains to the more experienced.

Cotoneaster horizontalis with fine spring foliage and pink buds about to open. A low-spreading shrub with distinctive branch growth, it is a popular and rewarding variety available from most nurseries. The moss on the surface contributes to the impression of trees growing in the open.

The Japanese recommend taking embryo bonsai from the wild in spring, a sound general guidline which must be tempered by climatic variations. If you are unsure which is the best month for lifting trees in a particular area, experiment first with garden seedlings, and always bear in mind the possibility of late frosts. Exactly how to dig up a wild tree and the first steps in preparing it to be a bonsai are described thoroughly in Project 2.

GROWING FROM SEED

Digging up trees from private land without permission is clearly illegal and, in a conservation-conscious age, uprooting any wild plant may be considered anti-social. However, there is usually no objection to the collection of seeds which have fallen from trees — a process which is actively encouraged in countries where the tree population is fast being reduced both by the demands of industry and the effects of disease. An autumn visit to any wood, park or even your own garden, will yield a varied assortment of seeds which can be grown into bonsai. If you prefer a wider variety of seeds than can be easily collected, you can buy tree seeds from the selections offered in the catalogues of general nurseries. In this way you will obtain a good selection of hardy and more exotic species quite cheaply, as well as receiving some basic information about the trees' characteristics and attributes.

One of the most exciting aspects of growing bonsai from seed is the possibility that the seedlings might show different characteristics from their parents — perhaps a degree of variegation, small leaves, or an interesting growth habit. You must be prepared, however, to have a little patience while the seeds germinate, and to restrain your enthusiasm for training during those early years while the baby bonsai are becoming strong. Concentrate your training efforts during this time on the more mature trees in your collection, and use the young seedlings to learn about feeding, watering, branch development, and general growth habits.

It is useful, though not essential, to be able to recognize different types of seeds as not all will be found close to the parent tree. When collecting, use individually labelled bags for different types of seeds, then plant the contents of each bag separately to avoid uninvited 'cuckoos' among the resulting seedlings. Utilize your seed container fully by planting together several dif-

Left: The shrubs on page 24 six months later, bearing the berries and leaves for which this species is prized. The fine, evenly spaced training wires on the branches can here be seen more clearly.

Right: Commonly available seeds which can be used for growing as bonsai:

Figure 11 Sycamore Almost a nuisance in private gardens because of its ability to grow quickly from self-sown seed, the sycamore is useful to bonsai enthusiasts because of that very same quality, although its leaves are generally too large to make good bonsai. The distinctive winged double keys, green when they first fall, then turning brown, are as easily spotted as they are grown.

Figure 12 Scots Pine Conifers are often more difficult to raise from seed than deciduous species and may take considerably longer to germinate. However, the small grey-brown cones are so easily available and recognizable, that it is worth preparing some seeds and setting space aside in the garden for them. The winged seeds are found at the bottom of individual 'scales' which make up the cone, and should be taken from a mature cone when it has opened in spring.

Figure 13 Beech A most attractive tree, the beech is particularly suited for training as a bonsai in that it has a good overall shape, with strong roots supporting a stout trunk and a handsome crown composed of many fine branches. The beech fruit or mast is a hairy brown husk which bursts open to shed its shiny brown nuts in autumn.

Figure 14 Holm Oak Although lacking the attractive, distinctive foliage of its deciduous brother oaks, this evergreen is a common, hardy species which bonsai beginners may find invaluable. Its acorns are very pretty, being small and stubby, usually virtually covered by the soft but knobbly cup.

Figure 15 Wych Elm Not to be confused with the ill-fated English elm which is well-known for growing from suckers, the wych elm is always grown from seed. Unfortunately, only a small percentage of the seeds are fertile, so it is best to sow many times more than you hope to raise. The oval, transparent seeds form before the leaves, are ripe in about May, and are borne off on the wind towards the end of June.

Figure 16 Field Maple The many kinds of maple, particularly the Japanese varieties, are very popular as bonsai, mainly because of their attractive foliage and thick roots. For those people wanting to grow maples from seed, however, the field maple is an excellent

ferent kinds of seeds which will grow in the same conditions. Bear in mind that sometimes only a small percentage of seeds will 'take' and so it is wise to sow as many as ten times the number that are needed.

Seeds fall into two very broad categories: hardy and tender. Hardy seeds can be sown out of doors without any special protection. (There are some half-hardy species which should not be put outside until after the frosts.) Tender seeds from houseplant and greenhouse varieties need heat to germinate and grow; but these should probably not be grown by newcomers to bonsai.

While it is perfectly reasonable to sow hardy seeds outdoors in temperate climates, provided

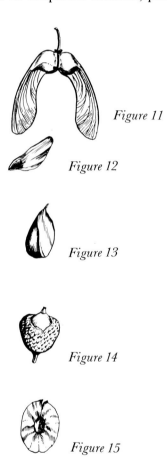

Figure 11

Figure 12

Figure 13

Figure 14

Figure 15

Figure 16

alternative to the more exotic imported trees, particularly as it has small leaves which have pretty autumn tints. Its winged keys, looking not unlike a squat airplane propellor, are a reddish shade in summer, but become brown as they fall.

that the ground is prepared properly, it is best to sow seeds intended for bonsai in seed trays or pots. Most seeds will germinate in a few weeks under natural conditions, although some coniferous varieties may take much longer than deciduous seeds. Ideally, sow in late autumn, winter or early spring when the seeds are ripe and fresh, soon after they have been taken from the wild or received from the nursery.

Seeds can be sown directly in prepared soil, but most benefit from one of the following treatments before sowing, to counteract dormancy. Generally, all coniferous and hard deciduous seeds, such as those of the hornbeam, which are very slow to germinate, are best treated before sowing; the most successful method is to place them in a cup of water in the refrigerator for two to three weeks, making sure that the water does not dry out. Then, on removal, plant them straight away, handling as little as possible. Similarly, the outer coats of such seeds as oak acorns may become hardened as they lie on the ground, and they should be softened before being sown by soaking them in warm water for a day or so. Seeds from domestic nut trees have a tough outer layer which can hinder successful germination and they should be chipped to help moisture enter. Do this with a sharp knife on the side opposite to where the seed was attached to its pod, so as not to scar the actual seed or 'nut'.

Many trees and shrubs which make successful bonsai, such as crab apples, cotoneasters and hawthorn, produce fleshy fruit which house several seeds. The seeds of such varieties can be removed quite simply by cutting open the usually soft fruit or berry. Seeds extracted in this way should be planted while they are fresh.

Seeds from tender species, such as lemons and pomegranates, do not have much chance of survival in temperate climes unless germinated and then raised in a temperature of 21−23° C (70−75° F), ideally in a heated greenhouse or alternatively indoors under glass in a propagator. Such seeds should be dry when sown but the soil should then be moistened with lukewarm water. Tender seeds need light and warmth to survive, but once reared, make attractive indoor bonsai which are hardy enough to be put outside during the summer.

All seeds should be sown in clean pots or seed trays which have been thoroughly washed and, if necessary, disinfected to prevent disease. Prepare the container in the usual way: cover the drainage holes with a layer of netting or some broken crocks and then add a layer of drainage material such as coarse sand. For large seeds old yoghurt or cream cartons may be used instead of individual plant pots, but do remember to punch holes in the bottom for drainage. .

The ideal growing medium for seeds is a mix of equal parts of good garden loam, sand, peat and leaf-mould, with a larger proportion of sand for coniferous seeds. Mix well, sieve and sterilize (see Chapter 5). (City dwellers should use a commercial seed soil mix.) Then fill the container to within about 1.5 centimetres ($\frac{1}{2}$ inch) of its top.

The depth of sowing depends on the size of the seed. Larger seeds should be planted a few centimetres deep, using a finger or a dibber to make suitable holes. Very small seeds need just a thin covering of fine soil, and the usual advice is to cover seeds with a layer of soil equal to their own depth. Put in the seeds, cover them with a layer of soil and firm down the surface, using the base of another pot instead of fingers, and then use a watering can with a fine rose to moisten the soil. Sow seeds sparsely; too many seeds close together can be attacked by a fungus which causes a condition known as 'damping off' which makes the bottom of young, overcrowded stems rot, though this can usually be avoided by the addition of a copper fungicide when watering.

Once sown, hardy seeds need only minimum attention. Simply place the seed trays outside in a not too exposed position but open to all weathers. If the seeds fail to germinate after a few months, do not try to force them by bringing them inside to a heated greenhouse. Leave them to the elements throughout the winter and most should come through the following spring. Do not despair even if there are no results after this time as it may be a couple of years before some seeds germinate. All you need do is ensure that they are kept moist, well aired, receive some warmth from the sun and are protected from predators such as birds and mice.

Some people recommend covering the seed tray with a piece of glass to avoid the soil drying out too quickly. Keep a regular watch on the trays to check for watering needs and signs of growth. Condensation should be wiped off the glass daily. As soon as the seedlings appear, take away the coverings and leave the trays in full light, but shaded from very hot sun, in a sheltered place away from draughts.

Do not be in too great a hurry to transplant the seedlings — hardy or tender. Wait until the majority have taken on a second pair of leaves, then carefully prick out the healthy ones and put them in small, shallow containers — individual plastic ice-cream tubs are ideal — in the same soil mixture as was used for sowing the seeds. At this stage it will be possible to inspect the roots. One main tap root will be particularly evident and so long as a good overall root system is developing, you can cut this back a little to stimulate further fine roots. Each time a seedling or plant is repotted, it is important to water the soil thoroughly, and keep the hardy species in partial shade until they are re-established.

Although it is unwise to attempt any drastic alterations to tender young trees, some preliminary training can be considered as they put on growth. Pinching out the tip and gently pruning the side branches, for instance, will lead to the desired bushy growth. After a year or two the little tree should be sufficiently established for you to work out what kind of bonsai is to be created. Young trees destined to be conventional size bonsai should be potted into larger containers to allow them to develop both root and branch systems. Trees intended for mame bonsai — up to 15 centimetres (6 inches) in height — should, however, be potted down into smaller containers to restrict growth after trimming back about a third of their roots. After watering, it is a good idea to keep such tiny trees moist by sinking the pots in damp sand or peat. After about another year, most trees will have developed enough to accept conventional training methods such as wiring. Gentle pruning, as before, should be continued to create the heavily-branched growth of a mature bonsai.

This mame elm is under 15 cm (6in) high. Although tiny, the sturdy trunk with a well-developed twist indicates that this is a mature bonsai. It is shown to its best advantage in a miniature container on a special mame formal display stand.

BONSAI FROM CUTTINGS

Those who feel that growing from seed is too slow a method of reproduction can create new potential bonsai relatively quickly by taking cuttings from suitable trees in the wild. In general, a cutting is taken from the stem, leaves or root of the plant. Stem cuttings are the type which most concern us here. Soft-wood cuttings from the new season's growth can be taken as early as May, while semi-ripe cuttings from more established growth should be taken in high summer. Most bonsai, however, are grown from hardened ripe-wood cuttings taken in the autumn and brought on through the winter. The speed at which the cuttings begin to root varies with the species and climatic conditions. Young wood grows quickly but needs a certain amount of heat, whereas the slower-rooting, ripe-wood cuttings need cool conditions with some shade.

Conifer cuttings are much harder to root, frequently demanding high humidity, light and hormones, conditions which can be achieved in the home greenhouse but are not available to everyone. It is possible to grow hardwood cuttings outdoors in a cold frame, but they need a full year to become established with no guarantee of success. Most gardeners despair of ever being able to grow pines from cuttings. One tip for possible success is to break the new branchlet required but leave it attached to the parent tree for a few days before removing it. This seems to produce less resinous cuttings which sometimes take root.

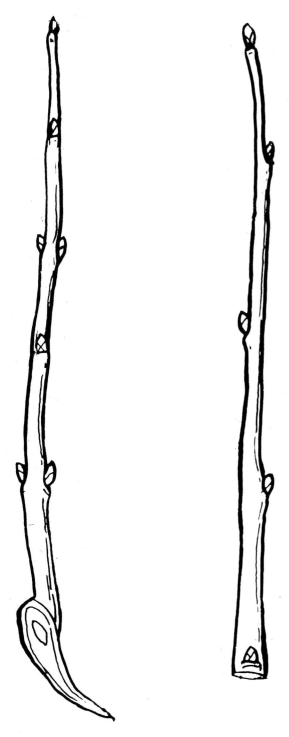

Figure 17 Heel Cutting This type of cutting applies to all plants with woody stems. Simply make a clean break of a fairly long piece of ripe wood, making sure that a 'heel' of the older wood remains at the bottom of the cutting. This will enable it to root more easily, as it has a wider surface area, although you will have to wait a year before seeing any signs of new growth.

Figure 18 Nodal Cutting When taking early cuttings from soft or semi-ripe wood, use a pair of sharp, clean secateurs to cut straight across the parent stem, about 8 cm (3 in) from the tip, directly below a node, or joint.

Willows are perhaps the easiest trees for the beginner to raise from cuttings but reasonable success can also be gained with zelkova elms and junipers. Larch, beech, oak and hornbeam all grow better from seed but cotoneasters, ivies and many flowering shrubs, such as lavender and escallonia, can be produced from garden cuttings. Though preferable to take ivy cuttings in summer, any time of year will do since these hardy climbers will root easily in nearly all conditions, especially if they are left in water for about a week before potting. Take the cuttings from woody growth, avoiding new shoots which are too weak.

The majority of cuttings should be potted straight away. Although growing from cuttings is a relatively simple process, certain basic steps should always be carried out to ensure success. Use a sharp knife or a good pair of secateurs for soft-wood and semi-ripe cuttings. Cut straight across the chosen shoot, just below the node — the joint where the leaf is inserted into the stem — taking a cutting of about 8 centimetres (3 inches) long. Ripe-wood cuttings up to 30 centimetres (12 inches) in length should be made with a 'heel' of the older wood attached at the base.

The best rooting medium for most cuttings is a horticultural sand, although the cuttings should be repotted as soon as roots have developed because sand contains very little nourishment. Before inserting the cutting remove all the lower leaves and dip the base in a hormone rooting powder, using the correct type for the kind of wood and following the manufacturer's instructions. Make a hole in the sand with a dibber and push in the prepared cutting to the required depth. Soft-wood cuttings should be inserted to about one third of their length. Hardwood cuttings should be inserted to about half or two thirds of their length. Press the cutting firmly so that it is quite settled with some soil around the base and then water.

Soft-wood cuttings should be kept moist and under glass. Greenhouse conditions of high humidity and bench heating are ideal but if these are not available put an inflated polythene bag over the cutting and container, spray the cuttings inside — not overwetting the soil — and then tie the bag securely round the pot to prevent loss of air and moisture.

Hard-wood cuttings can be planted outside but they should be placed in the shade, though not in too dark a position as the young plants must have some sun to survive. Do not feed until

Mame bonsai of different styles complement each other when displayed together. The ivy cascade, a perfect bonsai to train from a cutting, falls away from its tall container, while the informal upright cypress stands protectively by, its air of sturdy dependability being reinforced by the mounded soil at its base.

it is obvious from new growth that the plants have established a root system and then only in very diluted quantities. Over-fertilized soil can cause the young roots to burn, killing the plant. As soon as the root system is obviously well established, the cuttings can be transplanted and preparatory training begun as with young seedlings.

Trees that readily produce suckers from their roots, such as holly, acacia and wisteria, provide an easy method of raising stock. Suckers will have sufficient roots to live independently after about two growing seasons. The parent root should be severed with a sharp tool, immediately in front of and behind the sucker and the sucker carefully transplanted to a nursery bed or training pot to improve its root system before bonsai training is commenced.

31

Tools and Containers

TOOLS

Just as the majority of processes involved in creating bonsai are common horticultural practices many of the tools used on bonsai have their equivalents in everyday gardening and house-plant care. While the best tools are Japanese and consequently expensive − but so beautifully designed that handling them is a pleasure in itself − cheaper, home-produced versions can be substituted for some of the less essential equipment, and any good make of trowel or spade, say, can be used when necessary.

For the beginners who would like to experiment with working with bonsai before committing themselves to any expensive items, the only essential special tool is a Japanese bonsai cutter for branch pruning which gives a concave cut as opposed to the flat cut of ordinary Western-style secateurs. These are available in most countries through specialist suppliers whose addresses are obtainable from local bonsai clubs. Anyone seriously contemplating growing bonsai should probably purchase a half dozen basic Japanese tools including a pair of fine wire cutters with an especially strong tip; two pairs of scissors (the finer, longer ones for delicate work on leaves and twigs, the heavier for coarse work such as root cutting); a small rake, looking like a bent fork, with tines for teasing out roots and a spatula at the other end for flattening soil; and a chopstick for poking down soil to ensure that it goes between roots during potting. While being extremely strong, all these tools have an easy, loose action which makes them simple to use, even for people with little strength or grip.

All other basic items can be obtained from conventional sources. A pair of tweezers for bud removal, a pair of secateurs, and a spade, fork and trowel for taking trees from the wild are indispensable. Also necessary are a water spray and a supply of fine meshed man-made material for sieving soil and covering drainage holes in pots. Sheets of polythene and balls of string are needed when moving wild trees and a proprietary tree-pruning compound is useful for paint-

Left: A selection of unglazed earthenware bonsai containers in shades of brown. The range of shapes and sizes, all related to different species and styles, indicates the complexity of selecting the right pot for each tree. Note that several of the containers are quite deep, especially suited to the cascade style.

Below: A selection of the most useful tools for bonsai training. Top row, left to right: two of the many different sizes of scissors for trimming buds and branches, secateurs, wire cutter, branch pruner. Bottom row, left to right: trowel, jinning tool, fine hair brush, chopstick, trowel, fork.

ing over large cuts so that they will heal safely.

More specialized Japanese equipment relates to advanced work and, as such, does not really concern the beginner. A jinning tool, for instance, which looks like a pair of pliers, is used to create a deadwood effect by stripping bark, but should not be used by the inexperienced. Clamps, too, for keeping steady pressure on branches over a long period, can cause damage in the wrong hands. Carving tools for advanced work can be substituted with Western equivalents if need be, as can a grafting knife. And, while a brush for surface cleaning might be useful, it is not vital. This also applies to various different shapes and sizes of pruners and scissors. A turntable is useful for working on large trees from different angles and Japanese models are well designed, with a brake to fix the turntable at any point. Beginners would probably do quite well, however, with a much cheaper cake icing (decorating) turntable, the only drawback being its lack of a brake mechanism.

As with all garden implements, bonsai tools should be well cared for, cleaned after use and stored in a safe, dry place. Though initially expensive, Japanese tools will retain their qualities throughout a lifetime's use and are worth saving for from the outset.

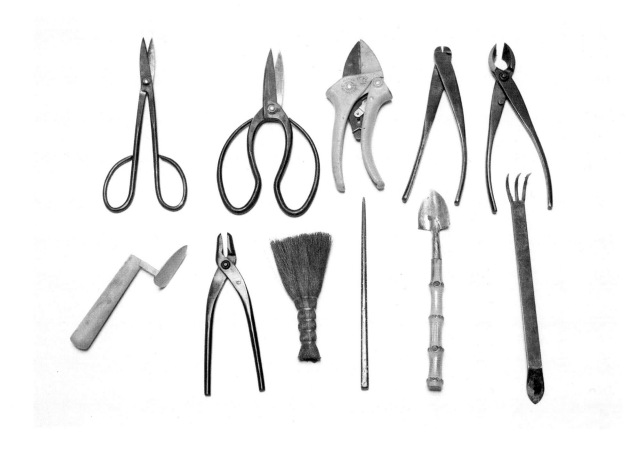

CONTAINERS

As the right frame sets off a beautiful picture, a suitable container complements and enhances a good bonsai. It would be a pity to negate the impression of a fine miniature by keeping it in an old plastic pot or some other makeshift container. The correct type of pot of the appropriate size, shape and colour for its tree plays a vital part in the overall aesthetic effect of any bonsai.

The relationship of an individual mature bonsai to its container is based on certain principles. Generally the thicker the trunk the deeper the pot, except for extremely short, thick-trunked trees which need shallow containers. Ideally, the diameter of the base of a mature trunk should be equal to the depth of the pot: the tree height, excluding the crown, should equal six times the trunk diameter (see figure 19). It must be stressed, however, that these are only guidelines to be taken account of, though not necessarily adhered to, as many fine bonsai are exceptions to general rules.

At the same time it should always be remem-

Mixed glazed and unglazed bonsai containers, including tiny mame pots, of various colours. The colour of the container is as important as its shape in relation to the tree.

bered that the purpose of the container is not only to create a harmonious visual effect but also to provide the right facilities for growing healthy trees. It is essential to establish the correct size and depth of container for trees at varying stages of growth. Young trees with small crowns and correspondingly small root balls obviously need small, shallow pots, whereas larger trees with heavy tops require equally large containers to accommodate the spreading roots and to present a balanced visual appeal.

Drainage is all-important for any plants confined in small pots, so a bonsai container should have one or more good drainage holes according to size. Japanese containers are made of materials which in themselves allow for good drainage, and they usually have little feet which enables water to run away freely from the drainage holes. Imported bonsai pots also have the

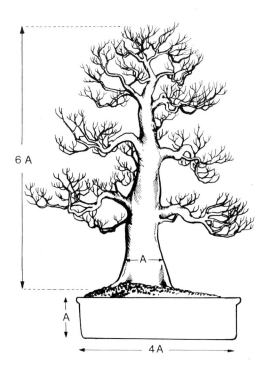

Figure 19 Showing the correct proportions of a mature bonsai and its container: the diameter of the trunk base (A) is equal to the depth of the container (also A); the height of the tree from base to tip should measure six times the trunk diameter (6A). It must be stressed that these are ideal proportions for a mature tree and should not be applied slavishly to young bonsai.

advantage of being virtually frostproof, essential in many climates if the trees are to survive hard winters.

Antique Chinese porcelain bonsai containers, frequently patterned, are very beautiful but are virtually unobtainable today. However, the Japanese produce excellent copies which are extremely long-lasting and represent a real investment. Indeed, because bonsai pots from Japan are produced in large numbers by automated process, they are only slightly more expensive than home-produced, hand-made containers, despite freight and import costs.

Bonsai pots are usually unglazed and of dull

colouring. The dark brown Kobe ware — named after its place of origin — is deservedly popular, while grey, charcoal and a more unusual greeny-brown are also seen. Japanese containers in dull greens, blues and reds are sometimes glazed on the outside, but never inside or underneath. Pale cream and plain white colours are less often found.

Different shapes and particularly colours of containers suit different species. Pine, juniper and other evergreens look best in an unglazed dark brown or dark grey-green pot, whereas deciduous trees with their more colourful leaves are shown to best effect in colours such as dull red, green or blue. The very small mame bonsai containers are unusually colourful, but because they are so tiny the colour does not detract from the tree or its surroundings. And, while patterned pots are rarely used for bonsai, some flowering trees do look especially fine in containers with a floral motif, so long as the colours relate to the blossom of the trees. Different styles of bonsai have their particular types of container too — cascades, for instance, are potted in tall containers and groups in shallow ones.

Knowing when and how to put trees in appropriate containers at their various stages of growth is essential if sound, balanced bonsai are to be achieved. A young tree in the initial stages of training, for instance, requires a container that will accommodate its roots without too much radical pruning. At this stage the visual aspect should not be overplayed as it does not really matter if the pot is a little too large for the tree so long as the root ball fits comfortably in it. When a tree has obviously outgrown its container, it must be potted on into a larger one. Trees undergoing preliminary training as mame bonsai may be potted down into a smaller container to achieve a finer root system which helps to ensure that the growth remains in proportion to the desired size. When tree and pot are balanced, repot the tree when necessary into its own container, but with a supply of fresh soil.

Caring for Bonsai

POTTING

Assuming that it is the right time of year, and that the bonsai is in good condition but ready to be moved to another container, the new pot must be prepared. Before putting a layer of drainage material in the bottom — fish-tank gravel is usually quite adequate, although the size and depth of the chippings must relate to the tree and the container — cover the drainage holes with a plastic fine-meshed material.

Then prepare the soil mixture. As soil in town gardens tends to be poor and lacking in essential nutrients, it is best for city dwellers to buy a ready-made variety. If garden soil has to be used, the inexpensive soil-testing kits now on the market are an excellent guide as to whether your soil is acid or alkaline. Should the soil be shown to have a high lime (alkaline) content, extra peat (acid) must be added if you wish to grow lime-haters such as rhododendrons and azaleas. Otherwise stick to those trees and shrubs which are quite happy in limey soil such as viburnums, lilacs, hollies and most conifers.

Always mix appropriate proportions of soil according to the type of tree. If you are not sure about the specific requirements of different trees, ask your local nursery or obtain the information from a good gardening encyclopedia. A suitable 'all-purpose' mix can be based on loam, enriched with added leaf-mould, sand and peat, according to the demands of the individual tree. But never add humus to soil in containers in a misguided attempt to 'feed from the roots', as it burns the delicate roots and encourages pests and green algae. Ensure that the soil is a little sandier than the tree would need in ideal conditions, as containers simply do not drain as well as soil in its natural environment.

Soil should also be free from disease. Sterile soil is essential in containers as trees so confined are unable to grow away from infested places as they can in the wild. The easiest way to sterilize soil is to put it in a tin with a well-fitting lid and place it in a hot oven at a temperature which will kill any harmful bacteria. Pouring boiling

Medium-sized bonsai on a Japanese display shelf. Top: Nishiki Japanese black pine, also known as 'brocade' pine has a rough, cork-like bark. Middle, left: Japanese winter berry; right: Japanese star jasmine. Bottom, left: Sargent juniper; right: needle juniper.

water over soil is, in contrast, messy and time-consuming as is using a disinfectant.

Sieve the soil to make it easier to work with. It should not be as fine as dust but of an easy running consistency, although much finer soil is needed in the tiny mame bonsai containers. The soil must be dry so that when the tree's roots are spread out in the pot, the soil will drop through them, ensuring an even distribution. Otherwise the root ball might end up sitting on a lump of damp soil with more wet earth simply heaped up on top.

When the new container is prepared, remove the bonsai from its old pot, taking care to handle it correctly: once the soil has dried out a little, turn the container upside down and tap it lightly on the base to release the root ball without undue disturbance of the soil; do not attempt to lift a bonsai by its trunk, as this can harm both branches and roots. Depending on the shape of the original container, the roots will have wound themselves in a round, square or rectangular mass. Carefully tease out the outer roots with a rake so that a smaller root ball with a heavy fringe remains (see Project 1, Step 2). Use a chopstick to remove the sometimes sour, un-used soil under the base of the trunk.

Trim off the excess roots with a sharp pair of scissors, but do not cut off more than a third of the root ball. If in doubt, err on the conservative side. If there is a thick tap root, cut it back a little with a pair of sharp, clean pruners and coat the wound with a healing compound. Put the tree in the prepared container.

As usual, there are general guidelines to follow in positioning bonsai correctly in containers. Draw two imaginary lines through the centre of the pot across the length and width, and place the tree behind the centre line, off-centre to the right or left (see figure 21). Tilt the bonsai slightly forward as this gives a realistic effect when viewing the tree from the correct, eye-level, position.

Do not plant the tree too low in its container. When it is in position, add more soil around the roots. Push this down between the roots with a chopstick rather than firming in with the thumbs. This is a lengthy operation but well worth the time to prevent broken or damaged roots and to ensure correct distribution of soil. Then slope the soil in a mound from just below the rim of the pot to the base of the trunk. This gives a natural, elegant look, featuring the roots which radiate out from the base. If you start the slope level with the rim of the pot, watering will

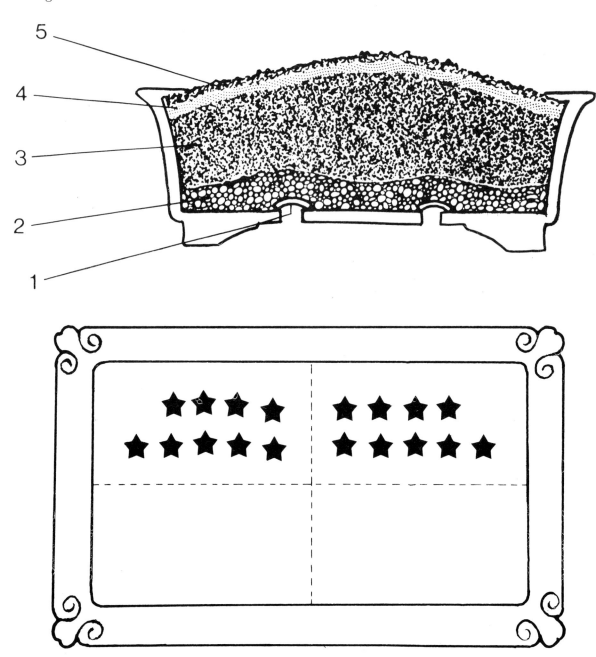

Figure 20 How to prepare a bonsai container for potting a tree: 1 cover the drainage hole(s) with a piece of fine-meshed plastic; 2 add a layer of coarse sand for drainage; 3 fill to just below the edge of the pot with the general soil mix, mounding the soil above the rim of the container in a gentle slope away from the sides; 4 pour over a layer of fine top soil; 5 finally sprinkle over dried moss which will grow when watered, forming a firm but springy surface.

Figure 21 Depending on its style and size, including the relationship of the trunk, branches and crown to the container, a bonsai could be placed in any of the 'starred' positions shown here. Note that the container has been divided into quarters, and that the tree should only be placed in the back half, always off centre to right or left.

be very difficult as the water will run down the slope and over the side of the pot.

Then press down the surface with a trowel, again not the thumbs, and sprinkle with dried, powdered moss which is commercially available and gives a natural effect when it grows. If potted correctly, the bonsai should now stand firm in its container. A tall tree which could be rocked by wind can be tied down to prevent movement while the new root ball is becoming established. Water thoroughly by standing the container in water to just below its rim. When the surface glistens, the soil is wet right through and can be taken out to drain. Then put it in a sheltered position, out of direct sunlight, before moving it gradually into full light.

Informal upright white pine in the classic pine style. This aged tree is in fine form, and has produced copious full-size 'candles'.

Detail of white pine, showing the healthy flowers. For details of how to prune pine by pinching out, see figure 28.

ENVIRONMENT

Good bonsai must be healthy bonsai. Sickly trees cannot be disguised by fancy containers. Trees, like people of different temperaments from different lands, require food and water, light and heat, in varying amounts according to their nature and general habitat.

Bonsai, like woodland trees, can usually adapt themselves to varying conditions but some cannot cope with extremes such as excessive cold and heat, wet or dirt. And, like their counterparts in forest and garden, different species of bonsai grow best in different soil conditions. Most flourish in full sunlight, although a few tolerate shade.

When considering the natural state of a bonsai tree, always bear in mind each one's different characteristics and limitations. Remember, too, that you are not dealing with outdoor specimens grown in their native earth but containerized trees which have some different demands from those in the wild. For example, trees growing in exposed areas, near the coast or on open plains, are subject to harsh winds which leave them permanently twisted and stunted, natural bonsai as it were, yet the same high winds would cause serious damage to trained bonsai which should always remain in sheltered positions.

Do not provide too much shelter at the expense of light, however, as most temperate trees grow best in good light. Bonsai enthusiasts who are also general gardeners may take a lesson from planting shrubs of supposedly compact habit under much taller trees: in an effort to reach the light shielded from them by the leaves of the trees, the shrubs will grow upwards in a straggly manner with only a few thin branches remaining at the lower levels. Note too, if you are a city dweller, how street trees lean away from the nearby houses and office blocks which give shelter and towards the middle of the road where there is more light.

Temperature too plays a considerable part in promoting healthy growth. Trees which thrive in hot, dry conditions, for example, can usually also withstand a certain degree of cold, but not if the drop in temperature is accompanied by constant heavy rainfall. In comparison, trees accustomed to a cool, temperate climate, do well in wet conditions but cannot cope with unusual summer drought. Extremes of climate are only tolerated by a few trees, such as pines. The novice bonsai grower is thus advised to concentrate initially on local, hardy trees.

WATERING

However well positioned, in full light with just enough shelter and average climatic conditions, no bonsai can survive without water, the most important aid to plant life. In the wild, trees draw on rainwater from the ground, initially using up water close to the roots then drawing it from the surrounding soil. Their roots may extend very deep to tap the enormous amounts of subterranean water so that trees rarely wilt, even over long periods without rain.

Bonsai employ the same system of obtaining water but obviously have only a limited area of supply. Once the little tree has used all the water in its pot and is sitting in dry soil, it will clearly die unless its supply is replenished. In fact, the soil should never be allowed to become bone dry. Water bonsai at the stage when the tree has begun to wonder, as it were, where the next water is coming from. Then water thoroughly, not simply wetting the surface, as otherwise the roots may grow upwards in their search for moisture and subsequently be burnt up in hot sun.

How and when to water bonsai is an art based on experience which can take a long time to master. Do not follow the 'little and often' maxim of so many houseplant enthusiasts, but only water when it is necessary and not before. There can be no set times or frequency. Simply observe the tree's appearance, test the soil with a finger and pick up the container to see how light it feels. In summer it may be necessary to water once daily, in winter once or twice weekly, but this depends on both the weather and the individual bonsai. Deciduous trees use up more water in summer than evergreens as their big leaves lose a lot of moisture. In comparison, the specialized foliage of conifers is better adapted to retaining water. In winter, however, the tables are turned: having shed its leaves, the deciduous tree needs very little water but the conifer, while remaining green although growing only a little, still uses water.

The hotter the sun the quicker the water loss. Yet even on a cold, overcast day, a strong wind can dry out a pot just as thoroughly as sunlight. Individual trees need different amounts of water. Pines, for instance, are very tolerant of drought, whereas fine-leaved deciduous trees such as the hornbeam or maple suffer greatly in hot weather unless there is correspondingly high humidity, conditions found in parts of Japan and the USA but not usually in Britain.

Regular spraying of the foliage of needled species, such as this juniper, is part of routine bonsai care.

The best time of day to water also depends on the time of year. In summer you may need to give bonsai water twice a day, in the early morning and in the evening when they are no longer in the sun. It is advisable not to spray the leaves if they are in the sun or if the sun will reach them before the water has completely disappeared since drops of water act as magnifying glass and can cause the leaves to become scorched. In winter do not water early in the morning when the soil is still frozen. If your bonsai needs water it is best to give it at midday, thus allowing the tree a few hours to use the water before the temperature drops again at night.

Rainwater is preferable to tap water which usually contains chlorine and lime deposits. If tap water must be used, fill the can some hours before it is needed so that the chlorine will disperse into the air. Indoor bonsai, particularly warmth-loving ones such as the calamondin orange, do not like temperatures below the 15–20° C (65–70° F) of average central heating, and should not be watered with cold water taken straight from the tap. Warm water is no substitute as it contains too much chlorine, so always keep a full can at room temperature to avoid administering cold shocks to the trees.

Trees do not like being dirty, particularly city trees which collect a build-up of soot and grime. Clean them regularly when watering, simply by letting water fall on the leaves. In general, water from above, using a can with a fine sprinkling nozzle or rose to prevent soil being washed away from the shallow containers. Only when the tree has been accidentally overlooked for a period and the earth become brick-hard should the pot be plunged in water to its rim for half-an-hour or so as using this method regularly tends to leach out vital fertilizers. Never stand bonsai in water for any length of time as too much water will rot the roots. Exceptions are, of course, willows, alders, swamp cypresses and other trees which normally grow alongside lakes and streams. Al-

The main feature of this 35-year-old beech is its sloping trunk, supported by a fine system of exposed roots, the whole giving the impression of a tree swaying in the breeze.

most all conifers, however, need very good drainage. Pines, in particular, are very sensitive to wet conditions and quickly develop root rot. Never forget that too much water can kill just as easily as too little.

FEEDING

One advantage of taking a tree from the wild is that the root ball will be surrounded by soil in which the tree already grows successfully. Where this is not possible, as when growing from seeds or cuttings, discover from a good gardening book or by observation the different types of soil favoured by different trees. As

previously mentioned, some trees must have an acid-based soil in which to thrive, whereas others might need an alkaline base.

Essential nutrients for healthy plant life exist in all except the poorest soils. As bonsai remain in the same shallow container for a lengthy period they tend to take out any natural goodness from their small amount of soil in a comparatively brief period. Since it is not possible to keep removing the tree to ever-larger containers with consequently more soil upon which to draw, the small amount of soil available must be given additional nutrients.

The vast range of fertilizers should be approached warily. They usually fall into two main categories: nitrogenous-based which produce green growth and phosphate-based which encourage ripe wood, fruit and flowers. The best fertilizers for bonsai, therefore, are rather low in nitrogen. Many of the chemical 'feeds' are reliable, though rather fast-acting, particularly in liquid form. Solid feeds are generally slower to

Laburnums, with their pendulous yellow flowers, make attractive bonsai.

act, as are the so-called natural fertilizers such as bonemeal, rape seed and fish-base, which can be advantageous. Japanese rape seed, although not commonly available, is recommended and often supplied by professional growers. It can be fed direct as a powder or put into a 'cage' especially designed so that every time it rains or the plant is watered a small amount of fertilizer is washed through into the soil. These are available from specialist suppliers. Never use a liquid fertilizer directly on the soil in dry conditions. Always wet the earth thoroughly first.

Err on the timid side when applying fertilizers and, if in doubt as to when the bonsai was last fed, let it rest for another period. On average, deciduous and coniferous trees are usually given fertilizer in spring to early summer and late summer to autumn, never in midsummer. Rest

flowering bonsai after the end of the flowering season. With a tree such as the crab apple which also bears fruit, do not fertilize until the fruit is well set or the 'apples' will fall off. When half grown, increase the feed till late autumn when the fruit drops. Bonsai which bear flowers and fruit should be given twice the amount of fertilizer as non-bearing trees, not simply in larger doses but by more frequent applications.

Repot flowering trees when they cease blooming. If a fruiting period follows, repot in autumn after the following year's flower buds have formed. Bonsai quince and wisteria should be repotted in autumn, and the cherry immediately after flowering.

PESTS AND DISEASES

The following two pages describe six of the commonest pests and diseases which may affect your bonsai.

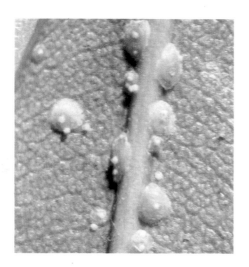

Bonsai suffer from the same pests and diseases as other trees, so always be on the lookout for unhealthy trees. However, perhaps because the little trees receive so much attention, most forms of ailment can easily be dealt with. In general, an occasional spray with a diluted branded insecticide is all that is necessary.

Found on houseplants and greenhouse plants as well as many fruit trees, shrubs and evergreens, the limpet-like scale insects inflict serious damage, often before they are discovered. The tiny, scaley creatures remain in the same place on the infected tree, exuding a sticky substance which congests pores. If possible, remove individual scale insects with a knife, but a general spray with malathion is also recommended.

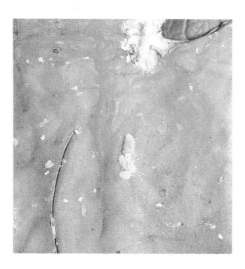

Sap-sucking mealy bugs, seen here on an oak leaf, secrete a white, cotton wool-like substance as a kind of armour. Mainly found on trees under glass or put outside in hot weather, they can weaken plants considerably by preventing them from 'breathing'. Clearly visible, the white bugs can be forced from leaves with a stiff brush or matchstick; the tree should then be sprayed with a general insecticide.

Another insect which covers its tracks with cotton wool-like blobs, the woolly aphid is found mainly on crab apples and pines. Easily discernible because of the white tufts, the greyish pest must be destroyed before it affects the trees so that a fungus is formed. Brush malathion or methylated spirits into the woolly blobs, and give the plant an overall spray with insecticide.

Almost everyone can recognize the ubiquitous aphid, the greenfly, which attacks all plants. Both young and adults are seen on this rose shoot. Greenflies multiply at an alarming rate, but fortunately can be dealt with comparatively easily, although they do tend to return if the conditions are right. Clustered together in groups on growing tips and young leaves, they prevent growth by sucking sap and also carry virus diseases from one tree to another. There are many branded varieties of insecticide spray to combat these destructive hordes.

The distinctive 'webs' of the tiny red spider mites are seen mainly on the underside of leaves and between the needles of conifers. These mites are particularly active in hot weather but are killed by cold. They attack many kinds of trees and seem to favour junipers. Their sap-sucking activities soon produce sorry-looking needles and mottled leaves. Spray at regular intervals as instructed on the insecticide container, as the mites can cause severe damage to bonsai.

Mildew affects several shrubs but is mainly associated with roses. Found generally in autumn when the air is moist, the powder-like mould can cause the buds not to open and the leaves to fall. It is very unsightly and debilitating. Spray with a fungicide, following the instructions given on the bottle or packet.

Pruning and Training

TRAINING BY PRUNING

Bonsai, like other trees and shrubs, are pruned to promote vigorous branch growth. The main difference in pruning, say, a full-size garden maple once a year and a bonsai maple throughout the summer, is that regular pruning of the containerized tree encourages a finer, twiggy branch system, thus giving the necessary bonsai proportions without harming the tree. Knowing when and where to prune bonsai can be learned through judicious reading, but only practical experience can teach the finer points of the art.

Whereas a tree just lifted from the wild should be pruned immediately so as not to give too much work to the damaged roots, a tree ready for initial training as a bonsai must be growing well with an established root ball. If you have obtained a healthy but unkempt tree with potential, first decide what sort of effect is to be created — a young-looking tree with upward-pointing branches, a mature one with downward sweeping branches or a twisted, gnarled old-looking bonsai. Then, bearing in mind that the main purpose of training is to flatter inflexible items such as the trunk and base, work out a plan of campaign, always keeping in mind the overall finished effect that is desired.

While Japan's strict bonsai practitioners observe certain rules in creating their tree shapes (see figures 1—10 in Chapter 1), these are not followed so closely in the West. That certain basic principles are adhered to, however, has already been noted. In particular, bonsai should always be viewed from the same position, usually with the trunk leaning slightly forward, and branches should be roughly alternate up each side of the trunk and to the rear except at the top where they are small and point in all directions. As bonsai are ideally viewed at eye level, what are known as eye-poking branches — those sticking straight out in front of the tree over the lower two-thirds of the trunk from the container — should be avoided.

Begin by removing those branches either wrongly placed or badly shaped which are superfluous to requirements. It is best to use the correct branch-pruning tool to create a concave

An informal upright ginkgo biloba. The 'Maidenhair Tree', as it is commonly known, is one of the world's oldest trees. Once thought extinct in the wild, it has recently been found in China. This tree, with its yellow autumn leaves, is hardy and survives in most soils.

cut in the trunk so that the bark grows over flat, leaving a smooth scar instead of an ugly lump. If such a pruner is not available, simply cut the branch off flush to the trunk and carve out the circular scar a little so that the bark will grow more easily over the hollow.

Then begin work to achieve a good overall shape and a finely branched structure. In most alternate-leaved deciduous trees — conifers will be dealt with later — this is generally achieved by branch or twig pruning, snipping off the offending part above a downward-facing bud. Remember that most tree branches drop with age so that upward-shooting ones rarely look natural. Always prune to an underneath bud for a downward-pointing branch (see figures 22—23). It is also difficult to train a branch into a good shape when it has been pruned previously to an upward-pointing bud (see figures 24—25).

Exact methods of branch training depend on what the grower has in mind as the final result. An ideal branch should taper in thickness from the trunk to its tip. It should not be very thick for three-quarters of its length and then taper almost to nothing, leaving only a tiny shoot to continue growing, which can happen as a result of over-severe pruning. If an existing branch needs opening up, do not complicate the procedure by working from an inward-pointing bud but find an outward-facing one. Where buds are not required to produce new shoots, say on the inside of a V-shape, simply rub them off, thus preventing scarring and putting strength into the area remaining.

Once established, many deciduous trees such as hornbeam, maple, the zelkova elms and cotoneaster, are happiest with regular trims, about once every two weeks during summer. Zelkovas, for instance, grow long shoots with several alternate leaves, but by regular light pruning with sharp scissors, a much-branched system will be created which quickly leads to a fine bushy tree.

An alternative method of creating the same type of bushy shape on deciduous trees is by leaf pruning (see figure 26). If a healthy, well-shaped maple is virtually defoliated at about the beginning of June, it will remain about the same size but develop fine twiggy growth. A smaller, more appropriate bonsai set of leaves will result, usually showing a bonus of more glowing autumn colour. Trim away all the leaves so that only the stalks, or at most quarter of the leaf, remains. As the stalks fall off, new buds and

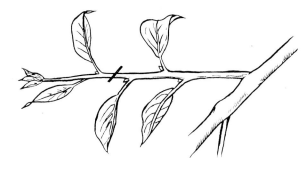

Figure 22 The correct way to trim a branch or twig of a deciduous tree to achieve the desired shape: with the correct branch pruning tool or, in the case of very fine growth, sharp scissors, make a diagonal cut a brief distance from an appropriate downward-facing bud, in the same direction as the bud.

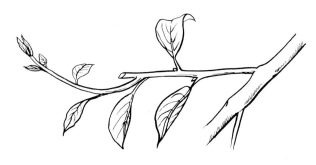

Figure 23 The effect of correct pruning: the new shoot will grow out from the bud in a graceful curve. Note that the extra piece of the old branch, left over by pruning some distance from the chosen bud, will eventually die back leaving a smooth joint.

Figure 24 The incorrect way to prune: as the usual intention is to promote downward shaped branches to create the impression of a mature tree, never prune diagonally upwards after an upward-facing bud.

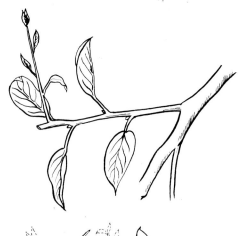

Figure 25 The effect of incorrect pruning: new growth shoots upwards at too steep an angle, and the end result is unnatural and displeasing.

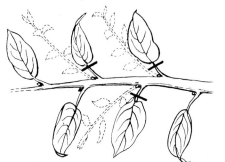

Figure 26 Leaf pruning deciduous trees may appear a somewhat drastic step, but if the tree is properly prepared and carefully attended to afterwards, this type of pruning will result in a finer, denser growth of smaller foliage. Use a pair of scissors to cut back all leaves to the stalk, then spray with water and keep in a sheltered place until the stalks fall off and new buds appear.

Above: The crab apple is favoured as a bonsai in Japan. This is a splendid example of an aged informal upright bursting with blossom in late spring.

Right: A close-up of the same crab apple. Its delicate white blossom is the same size as that on a full-grown tree.

leaves will grow. Only do this type of pruning if the tree is healthy, and give it a helping of fertilizer first to combat the shock of a complete trim. Keep the tree in shaded light until new growth is formed. It is not advisable to leaf prune in very wet weather.

Avoid over-pruning flowering trees such as the crab apple, as they then put on so much growth that in order to retain a good shape it is sometimes necessary to cut back the flowering buds. Crab apple bonsai should be pruned as little as possible, and the novice owner of such a tree is advised to consult a good gardening encyclopedia for hints on when to prune in relation to times of flowering, advice which applies to all flowering trees such as pyracantha, laburnum and wisteria.

Certain bonsai are particularly sensitive to radical pruning and die back soon afterwards.

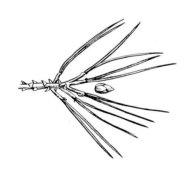

Figure 27 The correct way to prune evergreens by pinching out: here the new growing tip of a juniper has been gently pulled away from the old growth between the thumb and forefinger so as not to damage the remaining tip. Although the use of pruners to cut straight across the bud will not harm the tree irreparably, it will disfigure it for many weeks until it is hidden by new growth.

Figure 28 Pines can also be pruned by a variation of pinching out: in winter, simply knock off those buds which have already begun to form to make the following season's 'candles', and new buds will take their place to produce small 'candles'.

Here again, experience is the only reliable way of recognizing such trees. In general, however, those bonsai which do not come under the headings of flowering trees or summer 'nibblers' should be pruned twice a year, during the two noticeable growing periods of late spring and late summer. Bonsai beech and gingko come into this latter category.

A number of different pruning methods can be used according to the result required. Beech, for instance, should be pruned back as soon as the new shoot has extended fully, but before branch hardening has taken place, thus ensuring that secondary buds are formed in the remaining leaf axils. As beech normally produce buds near the tips of the shoots, pruning at a later stage would take away all the new buds, thus preventing further growth. You cannot afford to wait until the shoots harden and become woody, as secondary buds are already formed by this time, but must act on them while they are still young and soft.

The scale-like leaves of the members of the juniper family lend themselves to another form of pruning — pinching out the growing buds (see figure 27). By lifting out new buds with the fingers, an undamaged tip is left which encourages new side growth and a bushy layer. In contrast, cutting straight across with pruners results in an ugly brown tip which takes many weeks to be disguised by new growth.

A similar method of pinching out should also be used on the needle junipers (*J. rigida* and *J. communis*) with their spiky leaves. These produce new growth of tufts in spring and late summer. As the tufts are about to elongate, take out the centre part so that the new growth is encouraged from lower down (see figure 28). Japanese cedar *(Cryptomeria japonica)*, frequently trained into a formal upright style, should also be pruned by this method. They are fussier than the junipers, however, so care must be taken in estimating the right time to pick out the new tufts or else they will die back a little every time. As cedars need regular checking and pruning by this method, it is all too easy to restrict growth rather than encourage it.

Other evergreens need to be treated differently again. With some varieties of pine it is possible to knock off the buds (which would become

Another fine mature crab apple bonsai in autumn fruit. The spectacular full-size red berries hang from the tree like huge flaming lanterns.

candles in spring) in early winter, encouraging the tree to form other buds which then elongate as new smaller candles. If left undisturbed, pine needles would form from these candles, but if the candles are cut in half in late spring before needles are fully elongated, growth is made more compact and bud formation will also be stimulated. It is not always possible to employ both these types of pruning together. It depends on the variety of pine, its vigour and, of course, on the training policy.

TRAINING BY WIRING

Having pruned a potentially good structure, the next step is to put the branches in the best position, perhaps bringing them down to give an impression of age. This is generally achieved by wiring, an excellent training method if not abused, though one which frequently arouses controversy, mainly because many of today's commercially imported trees from Japan are scarred by wire that has been left on too long.

The essence of wiring is to use the correct tension. It is most important to learn to wire evenly with just enough pressure exerted to hold the branch in place. So as to provide a secure base, anchor the wire round the trunk (see figure 29). Too tight a wire will mark the bark very easily and wire that is too loose often results in branches bending and breaking in the wrong places.

Copper wire, which can be tempered by heating, is obtainable from most hardware stores and can be bought in pound weights of varying thickness. Do not use iron wire which rusts when exposed to the elements and marks the bark. Certain types of deciduous trees, particularly members of the cherry family, the barks of which react to copper and other metals, should be wired only with wire previously wrapped with paper. Plastic-covered wire is also available but can prove difficult to work with.

Remove the wire as soon as it looks too tight. If the branch has not set then it will have to be rewired. There is no reason why wire should damage trees if it is checked frequently. Anyone in doubt about how tightly to wire would be advised to take different strengths of wire and practise on garden trees and shrubs. Try bending these over a period to ascertain the thickness that suits each size of branch and the best time of year to begin such training. Remember that trees can be very brittle in spring and are likely to be damaged by wiring at that time.

The setting time depends on such factors as the size of branch, amount of bend wanted, time of year and variety of species. A small branch of a deciduous tree, for instance, might set in months or only weeks. Crab apple and maple, both fast growing, set relatively easily, as does pine, whereas a juniper branch might take two years to set. Some varieties such as cotoneasters and pyracanthas prove extremely hard to set if branches have been allowed to go woody instead of being worked on when green and sappy.

Wiring is in the end a matter of personal choice. If a branch looks wrong in its new position then it is possible to unwire it and put it back in its original position. It is not possible, though, to wire it in a diametrically opposed direction without putting the branch in real danger. This is because the water vessels of the branch stretch and may rupture as the branch is bent. In this way the branch may well die.

When wiring a large branch with only thin wire available, use two wires together, lying side by side, not crossed (see figure 30 e). Make sure there is enough wire to complete the branch in question, at least twice as long as the length to be wired.

Weights are not recommended for bending branches as they cause unnatural curves. They also make the branch swing about in the slightest wind which can lead to damage. Clamps are useful on bigger, thicker branches but need not concern the beginner as they have no place on young trees. It is perfectly acceptable, however, to move a young branch a little by tying it down to the container with string. Do not tie the string too tightly around the branch and do not tie at the very end of the shoot as this causes the same unnatural bend as a weight.

It is important to differentiate between the size and strength of a bonsai trunk and the size and flexibility of the branches. Branches growing close to the trunk can be pushed away from it simply by inserting a small wooden peg in the angle between the two parts. An old bit of branch is good enough for this and quite effective. It is helpful to trim the branch with bonsai pruners to give a concave shape to each end; these follow the contour of the trunk and branch to be trained. This method is especially useful for bonsai gingkos, which are never wired,

The crab apple bonsai, previously seen in full spring flower on page 49 is shown here having shed its leaves and revealing the splendour of its bare winter outline.

Figure 29 The correct method of wiring a branch to train it in the required direction. Prevent the wire from loosening and slipping by securing it to the trunk near the point where the branch grows out, then wind evenly and firmly round the branch to the tip.

Figure 30a Incorrect wiring. Here the wire is simply anchored in the middle of the branch, not wound round the trunk, and will consequently become loose so that it fails to hold the branch in the right position.

30b Despite being fixed to the trunk, this method of wiring is ineffective as the coils are too far apart to put the correct strain on the branch.

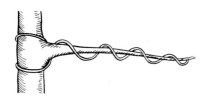

30c Wire that is too slack can cause the branch to break as it may suffer from uneven strain when bending. Conversely, too tight wire will bite into the branch, leaving ugly marks, or may even break it off where it joins the trunk by holding the branch too rigidly in windy weather.

30d Wiring over small branches, twigs, leaves or pine needles as well as the main branch will only scar these features so badly that the tree may well be ruined. Trying to wire two or more branches of different sizes with the same piece of wire is also incorrect and damaging. Wire only individual branches.

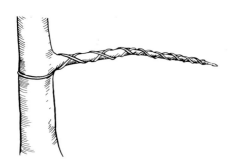

30e If wire of the correct strength for the size of branch is not available, do not try a short cut by using two wires crossing each other as here, or by twisting two together to use as one.

where numerous branches off the main trunk are to be trained into the candle flame shape. Pegging does not always produce quick results as the little wedges are often dislodged by birds or insects in the trees.

A wrongly wired branch is not necessarily a disaster. Simply remove the old wire and leave the branch for six months or so before wiring in a new position. However, a major error on a mature tree is not so easily glossed over. Here the best plan is not to try twisting the tree to the original desired ideal, but to 'file it away' in the garden. If it is frequently observed, perhaps turned around, tilted a little to the left or right, and if all the possibilities are considered, over a period of time a new idea will emerge and a new training plan can be put into effect.

Demonstrating the effects of bad wiring, this juniper branch is badly misshapen and scarred by the too-tight wire which has been left on so long that it has bitten into the bark. The remaining wire is old and rusty and should be removed immediately.

Overleaf: Six pleasing examples of different bonsai styles. Back row, left to right: Juniperus rigida in the driftwood or coiled style, a cypress cascade, and a white pine in the root over rock style. Front row, left to right: a hornbeam trained as an informal upright, a multiple group planting of Stuartia, and Chinese juniper in a five-tree group.

Project 1
Bonsai from a Nursery Beech

As recommended earlier, an excellent way to begin growing bonsai is to buy one or two young trees with potential for training as miniatures from a good general nursery (see Chapter 3). Many species fall into this category, including maple, cotoneaster and flowering shrubs such as azalea and laburnum. A wise popular choice would be one of the varieties of beech with its graceful structure, grey bark and bronze winter foliage. Being much in demand for hedging, beech is widely stocked by most garden centres.

One disadvantage of such commonly available trees, however, is that the sheer weight of numbers of any one variety in a single nursery can prove confusing to the beginner who may thus fail to recognize a good potential bonsai. To avoid this, whenever possible take along an interested friend who does not have preconceived ideas about what makes a bonsai and will see the trees with a fresh eye. Do not automatically reject those trees which, at first glance, seem hopelessly inadeqate for what you have in mind. For instance, a tree which has fallen over and remained on its side for a long time, may have developed a particularly one-sided branch system which could be trained as a cascade or waterfall bonsai. Above all keep an open mind,

concentrating on what the trees have to offer rather than what you would like to create, and you may receive a pleasant surprise.

At the beginning, however, you may opt for an informal upright style, perhaps the simplest shape for those first attempting bonsai culture. Although immature, the chosen tree should possess certain characteristics which indicate that it is good bonsai material. Look first at the trunk: a straight trunk, tapering gradually to the crown from a good, firm base is essential for this style. Avoid trunks with an ugly, waisted effect — a common fault in container-grown trees — or those with undesirable bends too near the base.

It is often difficult to estimate the length of trunk on trees such as cotoneasters which are nearly always well buried in the pot with lots of foliage spreading deceptively above. If in doubt, run a hand gently down the trunk to find out exactly where it meets the soil. If there is a reasonably long trunk, providing that other features are right, the tree may make a good bonsai cotoneaster.

Use a similar technique to assess the state of the roots. Sometimes plants are left too long in their original plastic or peat pots before they are transplanted into the larger containers in which

Left: The beech, purchased in early autumn, still in its plastic nursery container. About 30 cm (12 in) high, the little tree has a good long trunk which should thicken out well over the years. It also has a well-spaced branch structure which, although a little top heavy and one-sided at the moment, has potential for training.

Overleaf: The outstanding feature of this beech bonsai is its striking root formation. So strong and shapely are the roots that they appear as an extension of the trunk. The style of the top balances the tree's unusual base.

Step 1

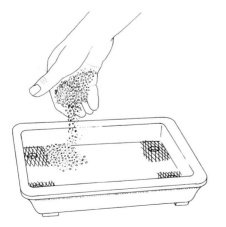

To prepare the new container, first cover the drainage holes with fine-mesh material such as the plastic garden netting which is widely available. Add a layer of drainage matter (as shown) such as fish tank gravel, obtainable from your local pet store. Use a soil mix recommended by the nurseryman, adding leaf-mould and sand as necessary according to the type of tree. Sterilize the soil and sieve it to a running consistency, then add it to the container.

Step 2

Take the tree and its rootball cleanly from the original container, either by cutting away the plastic or tapping lightly from beneath. Holding the tree firmly at the base of its trunk, shake off any excess soil and, using a small rake, carefully tease out any roots which have wound round themselves. If the root system is well developed, cut it back lightly all round so that a compact rootball with a heavy fringe of roots remains.

Step 3

Place the tree towards the rear of the prepared container, positioning it slightly to left or right of the centre line. If the tree favours the right, with its most prominent branches on that side, then put it on the left of the container and vice versa. Anchor it firmly in place with one hand, heaping up soil around the roots with the other until the compost is within 2 cm (about 1 in) of the rim of the pot.

Step 4

After six months or so in its bonsai container the tree has put on new growth, benefiting from the previous light pruning to develop a much more bushy outline. Marks indicate where the next pruning should be done to encourage growth on the side branches and keep down vigorous top growth which is undesirable.

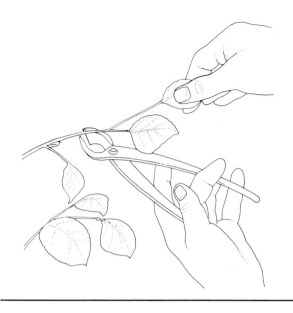

Step 5

To branch prune, take the unwanted part of the branch in one hand, holding it apart from the rest of the foliage so that you can see clearly what you are doing. With the pruners, snip off the over-length twig, just above an up- or downward-facing bud, depending on the desired direction of growth.

Step 6

The top growth has been cut back severely to enable the side branches to become stronger. Continue this regular light pruning until the tree has developed enough to be potted down into a smaller container, when the rootball will again be trimmed back. At this stage, in certain cases, the tree will become top-heavy in relation to its rootball, and should be kept in place by fine wires running over its base and through the drainage holes to be secured underneath the container, thus preventing it from snapping in strong winds.

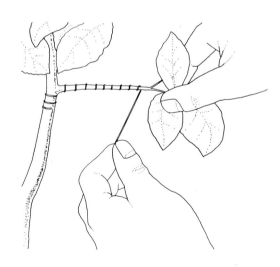

Step 7

When the young tree can be seen to be growing well and is on the way to a good overall shape, any wayward branches can be eased into position by gentle wiring. Here, a side branch is being brought down to give an impression of age. Anchor the wire round the trunk for stability, then wind the wire evenly round the branch at a regular distance, exerting just enough pressure to hold the branch in place. Setting time varies according to the season, species and size of branch being trained, but do remove the wire as soon as it looks too tight and rewire if necessary.

they will be sold. This means that the roots are unable to grow down and instead turn upwards, winding round and round the rootball so that eventually they become pot-bound. In a young tree, such circular roots can be unravelled with care, but they are virtually immoveable in a mature specimen.

Ideally, bonsai roots should radiate from the trunk base in a clear, untangled manner. As it is usually difficult to see the roots of very young trees, when a possible purchase has been singled out, poke gently down into the soil with an index finger; if you can feel the rim of the smaller pot still in there, do not buy that tree, however appealing. The nursery staff will not object to this amateur detective work so long as it is done in moderation and with care. They heap soil over the base of trees to retain moisture, particularly in large establishments where automatic watering is employed, so are not trying to hide the roots in any way.

Select a well-branched tree, not a single shoot. If you are going to create an informal upright style with alternating branches on either side of the trunk, reject trees with either branches growing opposite each other at the same level, with branches low down on the trunk, or with branches forming a cartwheel structure round the trunk. A common fault in nursery stock is a trunk with very few branches near the base. Although such trees might be perfectly acceptable in a group planting where a dozen or so tall trees would look very effective, it would be most frustrating for a novice to attempt to train one as an individual tree. In the same way, a branch too low down on the trunk will detract from its acceptability as a good bonsai.

Equally, a heavy top branch at this early stage will only cause long-term problems. It is relatively simple to encourage tops of trees to grow — a young tree will always look very upright as spreading only comes with maturity — but more difficult to make low branches thicken, so a tree which starts off top-heavy may only grow more so.

Having selected and purchased the tree, in this case a beech, carefully transport it home. However much you may itch to start work on it immediately, try to contain your impatience for a day or so and learn simply to live with the tree, studying its shape from all angles and deciding how best to tackle it. When you feel confident about the basic shape, give it a preliminary prune, cutting back over-long shoots to achieve a tidier overall outline. If you are trying to make

the branches grow down to give an impression of age, prune to an underneath bud (see figures 22 and 23).

After a week or so, when the tree has recovered from any shocks caused by the change of locale and the initial pruning, it can be transferred from its plastic pot to a more permanent home. Choose a proper bonsai pot so as to begin creating a flat rootball, but at this early stage use a fairly deep one which can accommodate the present rootball without too much radical pruning. Prepare the container as shown in Step 1 and described in detail in figure 20.

The simplest way to take the young tree from a plastic grow-pot, without disturbing the roots is simply to cut away the pot all around. If the tree is in an earthenware planter, however, allow the soil mix to become fairly dry then turn the pot carefully upside down and tap sharply on the base a couple of times to release both soil and rootball. *Never* attempt to lift any plant by its stem or trunk as it may simply break, or to loosen soil from the top as this may damage roots growing upwards.

With the rootball duly prepared (Step 2), place the tree in its container as shown in Step 3. Water thoroughly by standing the pot up to its rim in water until the soil surface glistens. Put the tree outside in a sheltered position, preferably in the shade of a larger tree but receiving some sunlight. As the roots become established over a three to four week period, the tree can gradually be brought into full sunlight. It should never again be necessary to water the tree by near total immersion, unless the soil has dried out completely due to unforeseen circumstances. Simply spray the leaves regularly to prevent transpiration and water only often enough to keep the rootball moist, as sodden roots tend to rot.

After a season's growth, prune lightly as shown in Steps 4 and 5. At this stage the container will still look too big for the tree, but health is more important than beauty in this initial period while the rootball becomes truly established. Years may pass before a satisfactory balance is achieved between tree and pot, by which time the nursery fledgling should be worthy of the name of bonsai. During this time, by regular pruning of rootball and branches (Step 6), repotting and training by wiring (Step 7 and figure 29), you will have learned far more by practical application than can be gleaned from any book. Now you will be creating more bonsai, in varying styles from different species

The young beech seen at the beginning of this project, branch-pruned and potted into a proper bonsai container, shows what can be achieved with basic knowledge and skill in 6—8 months.

and by extensions to the basic methods with which you are already familiar.

British and American bonsai societies are now actively encouraging the idea of growing native trees from nurseries as bonsai. However, it must be remembered that simply putting a tree in a pot and pruning it back here and there will not create a bonsai; only many years of careful training will result in the mature specimens which are regarded as true bonsai by the Japanese.

Project 2
Wild Pine Bonsai

Wild Pine Bonsai

Stunted, sinuous trees in the wild have already been described as Nature's own bonsai, their dwarf size and unusual shape being directly attributable to an alien environment caused, in the main, by poor soil and inclement weather. Such trees may also have been subjected to regular pruning by various animals in their search for food. However formed, there is little doubt that such shapely miniatures were the very first bonsai, being avidly dug up and cultivated first by the Chinese and later by wealthy Japanese who organized frequently perilous bonsai-collecting expeditions.

Although there is no need to go to such lengths today, selecting a wild tree to train as a bonsai can still be a fairly hazardous process, particularly in digging up the tree and ensuring that it survives, though the rewards can be equally great. Keep your eyes open for suitable specimens when walking through woods. You may not need to wander too far off the beaten track as stunted trees are often found close to the path, thoughtlessly trodden on by other walkers some years earlier and surviving in a misshapen form. Moorlands may also yield potential bonsai which have become stunted by growing in an exposed position. Look for young trees which will not object to being dug up and can only benefit from training. Do not be tempted by very contorted trees or those with lots of deadwood, as they are usually very old and will not take kindly to attempts to transplant them.

Many wild trees such as beech, larch, oak and pine can be trained as bonsai, provided that some precautions are taken when removing the tree from its natural habitat. Apart from the practicalities of obtaining permission to remove plants from private land, you cannot simply find a suitable tree one day and remove it the next, unless it is the right time of year.

The best time to take trees from the wild is just before their leaves are due to open, usually in spring, though the exact month or even week may vary according to geographical location. Never move deciduous trees when their leaves are unfolding as this nearly always kills them. If you have not been able to move the tree at the swelling bud stage, if possible leave it until the

Twisted by wind and weather so that its trunk and branches form a most curious yet harmonious whole, this Jeffrey pine at Sentinel Dome, Yosemite National Park, California, USA, is a stunning example of how the forces of Nature form bonsai in the wild.

same time the following year. It may well be, however, that the tree must be moved at a later time as the land is being cleared for building or agricultural purposes. In this case, dig up the tree, then take a pair of scissors and cut away two-thirds of every leaf. This lowers the rate of transpiration and puts less stress on the root system to draw up water. Do not take away all the leaf as cutting off at a node forces new growth which puts more strain on the roots.

The Scots pine, taken from its natural home and its rootball trimmed, has been potted at the start of its bonsai training. The top of the trunk and the branches have been wired gently but it has not yet been pruned.

Conifers can also be moved with some success in late summer when the soil is still warm and the trees have time to grow a new root system before the winter frosts. It is not advisable to lift deciduous trees at this time, however, even though cutting back the leaves will increase their chance of survival.

When going on a tree hunting foray, take care not to disturb the surrounding area by driving vehicles over cultivated ground or damaging other seedlings with heavy tools and equipment. Depending on the size of the tree, you need a spade and fork or trowel, long-handled secateurs to cut an obstinate tap root and a pair of small secateurs to trim away other extra-long, thick roots. You will also need some wet sphag-

Step 1

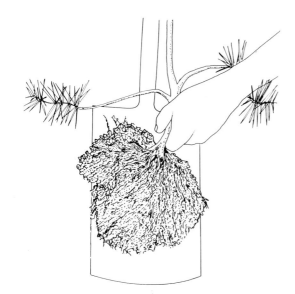

When taking trees from the wild, dig deep to make sure of obtaining a good rootball. Try to retain as much soil as possible, taken from deep in the earth where it is sterile and does not contain humus. Here the tap root has been cut back leaving the tree with a still large but manageable rootball.

Step 2

Prepare the pine for its journey home by placing it on a large sheet of polythene covered with coarse netting to secure the roots. Cut off any really long roots and pack damp sphagnum moss around the rootball to keep it moist over a long period.

Step 3

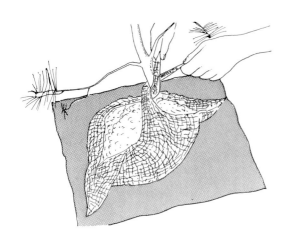

Tie up the rootball firmly but not too tightly and take the tree home as quickly as possible. On a long car journey, spray the leaves regularly to keep the tree cool. If it is very sunny, drop a polythene bag or sheet over the tree and spray beneath it from time to time so that the tree is enclosed in suitably humid conditions.

Step 4

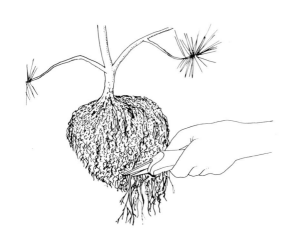

Before potting the tree, root prune gently to avoid further disturbing the roots, simply trimming any torn ones back to a clean edge. Even when trimmed, the rootball will be much larger than that of a young nursery tree and must be accommodated in a large container.

Step 5

Note how the tree is situated close to the rear of this deep plant pot. So long as all the roots fit easily into the pot, however, the position of the tree is not too important at this stage. Holding the tree firmly in one hand, make sure that the soil is well distributed around the roots, pressing it down with a chopstick.

Step 6

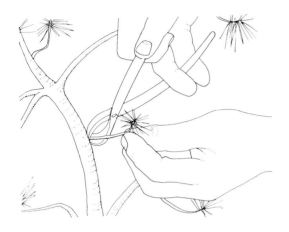

Cut off unwanted branches close to the trunk. Use of the correct Japanese branch pruning tool will leave a concave cut in the trunk. This helps the bark to grow over smoothly so that an unobtrusive flat scar remains instead of an ugly protruberance.

Step 7

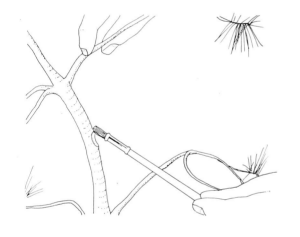

Help the scar to heal quickly and avoid infection, particularly if the cut is a large one, by painting the 'wound' with a special compound. The branded variety used on outdoor fruit trees after pruning is perfectly acceptable. Pines, however, may bleed when cut so soon after being uprooted and, in this case, the 'wound' is best cauterized.

Step 8

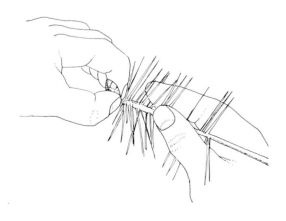

An effective method of pruning conifers when once the basic shape has been established is by pinching out the growing buds. Taking care to select the right branches, simply nip out the new buds between thumb and forefinger. This leaves an undamaged tip and encourages side growth. Do not cut across the tip, as this leaves an ugly brown stump which takes time to recover and restricts more useful growth.

num moss, a large piece of polythene, and string to tie up the tree securely for safe and easy transportation.

On site, clear away surface rubbish from around the tree then, looking down on it, mark out a circle about the size of the tree's crown. It is remarkable how deep even young roots may go, so dig well down around the circle to free the rootball (Step 1). Take care to inflict as little harm as possible to the roots and branches, securely parcelling up the tree for its journey home and creating a moist environment for it, as described in Steps 2 and 3.

A wild tree should be potted as soon as is feasible to minimize the shock of its being taken from the ground and moved. First, cut back any remaining taproot and other extraneous shoots, leaving a border of smaller roots around the rootball. The main object now is to keep the tree healthy while it develops a new root system, so do not attempt to restrict the rootball within a conventional shallow bonsai container but prepare a suitably large plant pot or deep seed box, retaining as much of the original soil around the roots as possible. The remaining soil should contain a mixture of ingredients — peat, loam, leaf-mould, etc. — particularly suited to the type of tree. For instance, a preponderance of sand in the soil mixture will be appreciated by pines.

Pines are popular bonsai trees the world over. The Japanese white pine *(Pinus parviflora)* is much used in that country as it adapts so easily to the classic pine style and many others. In Britain, the Scots pine *(Pinus sylvestris)*, as used in this project, is a common bonsai tree, but it needs handling with special care when taking from the wild as roots may 'bleed' when severed and should ideally be cauterized if the pine is to survive with any degree of success.

When the wild tree is securely potted in its temporary container, to help the roots re-establish themselves in their new home in the shortest possible time, take away part of their workload by removing any branches which are superfluous to the basic shape, as in Step 6. If you do not have a proper branch pruner which makes a concave cut, simply take the branch off flush

The incredibily curved trunk of this blossoming hawthorn has the extravagance of the wandering literati-style bonsai. The excessive trunk was formed in the wild, where it was found growing beside a windswept path, then potted and trained as a bonsai.

After a year, the pine from the wild is beginning to look much more like a bonsai. It has been pruned regularly to achieve a more compact shape, though the branches remain wired to bring them down more in keeping with an older tree. It has been repotted and positioned against a large rock which is used as a feature to create the impression of the pine growing in a natural environment.

with the trunk, then use a sharp knife to carve out a circular scar. This will enable the bark to grow over as neatly as if a concave cut had been made originally.

The tree can now be placed outside and moved gradually into full sunlight. Conifers which have not adapted to their new home soon show symptoms of distress such as dehydrated needles. Make sure that such trees are in well-drained soil and increase the humidity by placing them in a cold frame or blowing up a polythene bag and putting it over them. Do not be misled into thinking that the trees need feeding as fertilizer will burn damaged roots which tend to rot in over-rich soil.

Depending on the individual tree, the time of year and the weather, it should start to put on new growth within a matter of months. Do not attempt to repot it at this stage as it can take up to a year for the new rootball to become established. A little light training can commence, however, after a few months, so long as the tree is obviously healthy. Wire any wayward branches lightly and evenly in place as described in Chapter 6 (figure 29). Think of the ideal shape in relation to the correct bonsai container and, if it helps, tilt the pot so that the branch is at the right angle before wiring.

Later, when potting down to contain the new rootball within the confines of a smaller pot, you may discover that the rootball and the wired branches are at very different angles, so that potting the tree in the usual upright position would only result in the branches being entirely misplaced. To avoid this discrepancy, trim the rootball and pot the tree at an angle so that its branches do not look too out of place. Then, when potting on to the final bonsai container in a year or so, the rootball can be positioned correctly and the branches should be well on their way to achieving the desired shape. Thereafter, all that is needed is the customary root and crown pruning, plus general care and repotting every few years, to keep the wild tree an acceptable, if not spectacular, mature bonsai.

Project 3
Rock-clinging Maple Bonsai

Rock-clinging bonsai are ideal for beginners who are already training one or two informal upright trees and wish to create new styles at the same time as learning different techniques. Relatively simple to produce, bonsai with roots clutching rocks look most impressive, recalling scenes of trees perched perilously on a mountain-side or above a cascading waterfall.

As the rock is the corner-stone of this miniature scene, it is well worth taking the time and trouble to build up a reserve of suitable pieces of stone. Large, jagged upright rocks are popular, but size is really immaterial as certain trees benefit from being dwarfed by their setting whereas others play a dominant role. Shape too depends on the impression that is being created: a long, relatively flat rock would be successful as a plateau or an island, and a rounder, taller one would perhaps best represent a hillside.

In general, rocks for use with bonsai should have interesting shape and texture and possibly colour. Look for them in old quarries and on any stoney ground, discarding very smooth stones, however attractive they may be, as the bonsai roots must have a rough surface to cling to. (Do not use rocks from the seashore unless they have been left to weather in a garden for at least two years so that all the salts have been leached out of them.) Porous rock is well worth searching for as it reduces the need for daily watering. And, whatever its other attributes, it is most important that the rock contains at least one cavity large enough to hold the tree.

Do not despair, however, if you find a rock of the ideal shape and size but lacking any indentations in which the roots can anchor themselves. Simply take a chisel and tap lightly with a hammer to chip away small pieces of the rock, thus making the necessary holes and 'ravines'. If confined to a city with no chance of collecting natural rocks, experiment with old bricks, cracking them in large pieces and again scoring the surface with a chisel. And, if all else fails, or you are seeking a definite shape for a particular effect, why not make it yourself from cement or concrete? In this way you can control size, shape and texture, and even drill holes exactly where the roots are to lie.

Many trees are suited to the rock-clinging style, so long as they can be persuaded to grow good long roots. Encourage them by planting the baby bonsai at the top of a deep container, as narrow as possible, so that the roots have plenty of room to go straight down and not wind themselves around as they would in a shallow

container. Those intending to produce several bonsai in this style might find it useful to construct a deep box with slatted sides which can be built up layer by layer as the roots extend. Beginners might prefer to utilize more mundane objects such as an old plastic bucket, so long as adequate drainage is provided.

When the roots have grown long enough to extend just below the chosen rock, it is time to decide how the rock should best be viewed to create the desired effect. Try to see how the tree will look in different positions on the rock. Do not automatically place it at the pinnacle or on an obvious plateau in the middle. A small tree, for instance, may look most natural if planted in a crevice on the rock side. When the best site has been found, hold the tree in place, spreading out the roots and cutting away any short ones which do not reach the rock base. You will need both hands to secure the roots in position, so tie the tree temporarily in place if it is at all unstable.

It is not advisable simply to spread out the roots and cover them with the clay and peat mixture (Steps 5 and 8) without first fixing them to the rock with wires. For this you will need several lengths of fine wire, about 15 cm (6 in) long, and a lead 'weight' to sink the wires in the rock cavities. Make your own sinker (Step 3) and press home the wires with a punch or nail (Step 4). Should the rock have a hard, smooth surface which prevents you from sinking the wires in this way, simply glue them in place with an epoxy resin adhesive.

With the roots anchored to the rock and placed in a relatively deep temporary container (Steps 8 and 9), it is a good idea to tie up the sphagnum moss with twine as this prevents the moss from being washed away in heavy storms,

Left: The roots of the trident maple knit together, to make this an ideal tree for training in a rock-clinging style. This maple differs from the more common Japanese maple in that its leaves are divided into three. Easily cultivated, it lives to a ripe old age, as demonstrated by these thick, gnarled, trunk-like roots. (The marks made by wires that were left too long are still noticeable on the base of the trunk.)

Overleaf: This fine Japanese maple in its autumn colours, was originally considered to be a rather flawed bonsai because of its forked trunk, despite its shapely crown. Growing it over a rock has made a feature of the split trunk which is still unusual, but looks quite natural.

Step 1

To train the young tree's roots to grow very long so that they can eventually cling to the rock, plant the baby maple at the top of a deep receptacle full of compost. A large plant pot or an old bucket make perfect containers so long as they have adequate drainage holes. Ensure, too, that there is a good layer of drainage material in soil of this depth.

Step 2

After a year or so when the roots have grown long enough, carefully take out the tree and remove all the soil from the roots. Find the best place for the tree by holding it in different positions on the rock. With the bonsai temporarily in position, spread out the roots over the rock and note where they can best be attached to the surface.

Step 3

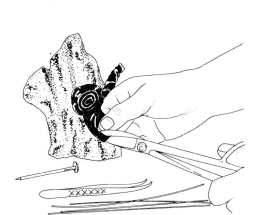

Use very fine wires to fasten the roots to the rough-textured rock. Secure the wires with lead 'sinkers', made by cutting pieces of lead foil — the weight of foil used on the tops of spirits bottles is best — in thin strip about 1 cm ($^1/_2$ in) long.

Step 4

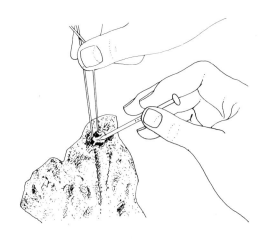

Fold several 15 cm (6in) lengths of the wire in half and twist the foil strips round the middle, bending them to the shape of the rock cavities. Position the wires on the rock so that they can be tied round the roots and use a long nail to push the foil sinkers firmly into the surface holes.

Step 5

After mixing together equal parts of clay and peat, use a finger or small trowel to push the mixture into the places in the rock where the roots will lie. This 'soil' mix, which should be wet but not runny, will give the roots something to cling to and feed on.

Step 6

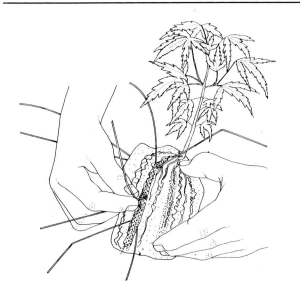

Position the tree on the rock and spread out the roots so that they hang over the crevices of clay. As it takes time to arrange the roots correctly, prevent them from drying out by spraying occasionally with cool water. Anchor the roots firmly by tying the wire round them as securely as possible, but not so tight as to cause bruising. Knot the wire and trim off any excess.

Step 7

With the tree and roots in position, take the remaining clay/peat mix and use it to cover all the roots from top to bottom, preferably to a depth of about 1 cm ('/₂ in). Do not skimp this operation, even though it is messy, as the roots must have some form of sustenance and cover.

Step 8

Prepare a container just slightly wider than the base of the rock and about a third as deep as the rock. Start with the usual layers of drainage material and basic soil mix. Taking care to lift the whole rock, rather than just the slender tree, put it in the container. Heap up the soil around the bottom of the roots and about a third of the way up the rock to protect it to that point.

Step 9

Pack damp sphagnum moss around the top of the rock where the roots are still exposed. This moss, which should always be kept moist with regular spraying, prevents the clay from drying out or being blown away.

It is possible to cultivate another version of the rock-clutching style by growing the trees actually in the rock cavities so that no other container is needed. This wandering holm oak (left), with the smaller branch coming off the trunk to the left, admirably suits this method, and the rough, shapely rock is a perfect vessel. The same technique has been used in the unusual decorative shell-shaped rock (below left) in which the roots of the jasmine are planted. To create the effect of a little garden, soil and moss are heaped up over the top and down the sides of the rock which contains water in the hollow so that the trees appear to be perched above a small pool.

or being blown away in hot weather if it has been allowed to dry out. Then put the container outside in a sheltered position, gradually bringing it into full sunlight as usual, but always protecting it from the wind. Apart from checking from time to time to see that the moss is damp, and occasionally spraying the leaves, do not disturb the tree for about a year. Once the roots have grasped the rock they must not be

separated or they will die, so try to resist any temptation to see whether or not they have taken.

After a year, the roots should have become established. The moss can then be removed and any remaining clay washed off, revealing the strong, sinuous roots attached to the rock. (If, on taking away the first lump of moss, it is obvious that the roots have not taken, wait a further six months or so before looking again.) The rock-clinging bonsai is now ready to be potted in a permanent shallow container. Prepare the container in the usual way and position the rock securely in it, covering the ends of the long roots with compost so that they have a firm base.

As the tree ages, the roots will continue to thicken until they become as strong a feature as those of the maple illustrated at the beginning of this project. Continue to care for the tree by the usual methods, employing pruning and training techniques as necessary and repotting whenever appropriate.

Project 4
Raft Bonsai

Raft bonsai, as the name implies, is a style where several apparent trees are anchored in a sea of earth and moss by a thick, platform-like root. If this single root is not prominent, the raft may sometimes appear to be a group planting in its own right, with sinuous trunks and full crowns creating the impression of at least a copse, if not a whole forest (see Project 5). Similarly, the less well-informed sometimes confuse raft bonsai with the multi-trunk styles popular in Japan, where twin, triple and even more trunks spring from a single base.

All three styles are, in fact, quite discernibly different: *individual* trees are planted to give a group effect; in, say, a twin-trunked bonsai, the two crowns are but part of one sub-divided trunk; whereas the essential feature of a raft is the single, long root. Perhaps the style closest to this is the root-connected bonsai, again more common in Japan than in the West. Such trees occur in the wild, blown over or uprooted in a storm but remaining alive although lying on their side.

Such trees respond to the dim light which is filtered through other trees, by throwing out those branches nearest the light to form individual trunks. The crushed branches on the other side die back and the old trunk itself puts down roots to support the new branch-trunks.

Mature trees of this formation can quite often be found in exposed woodlands, but it is unusual to find young root-connected trees capable of being trained as bonsai. The raft has therefore been developed as the man-made version of this natural phenomenon. In simple terms, the tree is potted horizontally so that the old trunk sends down roots and its branches grow up as new trunks. Eventually, as the old trunk thickens and sends down roots and the new branch-trunks put on more growth, a very impressive type of island bonsai is formed.

Be warned; a raft will take years to create, and once again it is best to have other trees to cultivate while the raft is becoming established and putting on growth. Also, if you are in a hurry, do not choose a wild tree. Although most wild species are capable of being trained as rafts, they do have a major disadvantage in that

Although it looks at first as if several junipers are growing together here, this is in fact a powerful raft bonsai springing from a single root. The tree is very old and has been subjected to some rather harsh training, or perhaps merely neglect. It is now being worked on to achieve its full potential.

they will possess a well-developed rootball. This large, usually round rootball will, of course, be superfluous when the tree is turned on its side to make the raft. Indeed, such a rootball frequently makes it impossible to begin a raft style straight away. Ideally, a wild tree should simply have its rootball trimmed to avoid undue shock after being moved, then be trained for at least a year in a shallow bonsai container so that it learns to survive with a smaller root which will be less bulky when training commences.

For this reason, it is better to pick a young nursery tree which has a less developed rootball and its branches will also be more pliable. Choose an upright species as spreading shrubs, such as certain varieties of cotoneasters with their many small branches and very small leaves, will not adapt to the raft style. And look for a tree with a relatively straight trunk as this will take root more easily when it is turned sideways than a sinuous trunk which refuses to be covered by the potting soil.

For once, you are not looking for a tree with a good potential shape, nor does it need to show signs of an abundant crown. Rather, so long as the tree is obviously growing well, it is preferable if the majority of its branches grow out straight from the trunk, favouring one side. It is these branches which will eventually form the new trunks.

Before lightly wiring the branches so that they are all pointing out from the trunk in one direction (Step 2), take off any which will detract from the raft's progress, such as any well-developed branches on the 'wrong' side and any skimpy ones on the preferred side which might not keep pace with the general growth. If any of the remaining branches are out of step with their fellows, say too long or with curved tips, prune them back so that they are all approximately the same length.

When first potting the raft, the aim is to encourage it to put down roots suitable for bonsai cultivation in the shortest time possible. You should therefore use a fairly shallow container, even if it looks quite bizarre at this early stage with about half the old rootball appearing above the soil at one end (Step 3). Some practitioners recommend cutting off the mass of the rootball to begin with so it does not show, simply burying the rest; but there is a chance that the raft might well die if deprived of the majority of its original roots so early.

Do not expect the new root to become established without any outside help. All trunks will

Step 1

The young larch, still in its plastic pot as purchased from the nursery, is a healthy but unbalanced tree. Note how the majority of its branches grow to the right, with only the odd thin one on the left of the trunk. Though possessing almost no potential for any other bonsai style, it is, however, the perfect type of tree from which to make a raft bonsai.

Step 2

With the tree remaining in its original container, gently but firmly wire the branches so that they are all pointing in the same direction, in this case to the right where the majority grow naturally. Begin wiring from the point where each branch joins the trunk, but do not wire around the trunk, as this is to become the root and it is well nigh impossible to remove the wire when once the trunk is rooted in the earth.

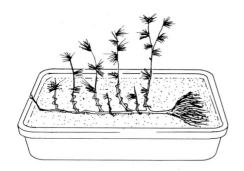

Step 3

Carefully take the tree from its pot and turn it on its side so that the trunk is now in position to become the 'root' and the wired branches to become little trunks. Fill a shallow wooden box, seed tray or bonsai container with appropriate soil mixture and pot the new raft in what would be a horizontal position for the original tree. As a result, the old round rootball will be at one end of the new trunk root, and part of it will stick up above the surrounding soil.

Step 4

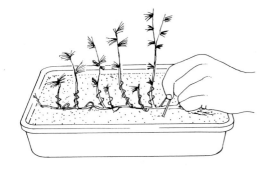

Make several incisions in the trunk root on the side that will rest in the soil and put a little rooting powder in each. Bend some short lengths of training wire in the shape of a hair pin and anchor the new root down in the soil with them, particularly in places where a curved trunk/root does not lie close to the surface. Pile up soil around the new trunk root and over the bottom half of the old rootball.

Step 5

When it is obvious that the raft has taken — as the little trunks put on growth and new roots can be seen under the top layer of soil — the old rootball will become superfluous and can simply be cut away. Do not be in too much of a hurry to repot the raft, however, as it can take between 1—5 years before it is sufficiently established to be put in its correct container.

Step 6

After this time, when the original branches are really beginning to look like individual trees and a mass of long roots have grown from the new root, the raft should be taken from its temporary home and potted down to a shallow bonsai tray. Holding the raft on its bed of soil, spread the roots out so that they radiate around the container and press soil particles in between them with a chopstick. Add more soil, building it up into a mound from the sides of the tray to the centre and thus displaying the raft to its best advantage.

The same raft bonsai as the one shown on page 84 here demonstrates the benefits of care and attention.

root quicker if treated as in Step 4. Do not make too many cuts or too deep and only apply a little hormone rooting powder. If the trunk curves away from the soil and does not remain firmly in place with thin stands of training wire, a few bent hairpins should do the trick. In a mature raft, like all "multi-trunk" bonsai styles, ideally no tree should align directly behind another when viewed directly from the front or from either side.

When the raft is firmly potted it can be put outside in the usual sheltered and partly-shaded position, then left for as long as it takes the new root to grow. Throughout this time, check the tree occasionally to see that it has not dried out or been knocked over and that it remains healthy. Water as required, but otherwise forget about the tree until such time as the new roots are showing through and you can happily dispense with what is remaining of the old rootball (Step 5).

It will then be an even longer period before you can pot the raft in its bonsai container (Step 6), certainly a year or more depending on the species. However, this does not mean that you should leave the raft entirely to its own devices for this length of time. As soon as the branches begin to thicken, taking on a more trunk-like form, they can be lightly pruned to whatever shape you have in mind. When these trunks are all growing up sturdily towards the light, you can take off the preliminary wiring on some and wire others into more natural forms so that the raft begins to adopt a more realistic shape instead of growing straight up like a row of soldiers.

The raft will remain in its first true bonsai container for several more years before it is ready to be potted down. Continue leaf and branch pruning and rewiring, as necessary, throughout this period. When a firm, flat root-ball is evident, this should be root-pruned and the raft potted into a shallow tray. Build up the soil from the sides to the plateau that is the root, so that the island-like qualities of the raft are all the more apparent.

Project 5
Group Plantings

Above: Photographed in the autumn, this is the same zelkova group as that on the left in spring.

Left: This fine group of three zelkova elms in full spring foliage look like a little copse through which the viewer is about to walk. This effect is achieved by placing the tallest tree at the back of the group and the smallest at the front.

Group plantings are a popular bonsai style, mainly because it is fairly easy to achieve an attractive forest-like profusion without too much effort and by use of comparatively inferior trees. The overall shape of a group is more important than the shape of individual trees, so that immature trees which are not sufficiently developed to stand alone as bonsai can be used to good effect. Indeed, if correctly positioned, several small young trees can look like one big, old specimen, and the effect is even more impressive when trees of different generations are combined so that, say, one mature bonsai is surrounded by young trees.

Many people also find group planting fairly

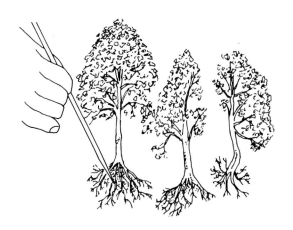

Step 1

Prepare an uneven number of trees — in this case three zelkova elms — of sufficient size and similarity for a group planting. Ideally, all the trees should have been trained as bonsai in shallow pots for at least a year to grow relatively flat rootballs. Before potting, tease out the roots with a chopstick to unravel them and prune gently all round until a light fringe of roots remains, then spread these out evenly from the trunks.

Step 2

Choose a bonsai container large enough to accommodate however many trees are being used, of the correct shape to achieve the desired effect and prepare it in the usual way. Here, a woodland copse viewed close up is to be created in a relatively small, round pot of sufficient depth. Having pinpointed the position of each tree in relation to the rest, with the tallest at the rear, contour the soil accordingly. Press the soil down with a chopstick, a time-consuming process but one which gives a very firm base.

Step 3

As is always the case when trying to portray a close-up scene, pot the main tree towards the back of the container and continue heaping up the soil around its base. The remaining trees will be on slightly lower ground, in descending order, the whole impression being of a copse in a mountainous landscape, somewhat isolated from the rest of the forest.

Step 4

Here, the second sized tree has now been positioned slightly to the front and to the left of the tallest one. Now put the smallest tree in place, nearer the front rim of the container and a little to the right of the centre tree. The three zelkovas, as shown in the illustration opposite, are not symmetrical but form an unequal triangle with the steep right-hand side shorter than the sloping side. Ideally, when viewed from above, two of the trees on one side of the triangle should be close together, with the third some distance apart.

Step 5

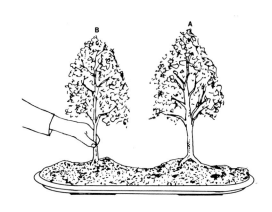

A larger group of eleven zelkovas is to be created, incorporating the previous three. Now the aim is to give the impression of a larger forest seen from a distance. The original group thus cannot remain in their present position as they must relate to the additional trees in size and placement to achieve the correct perspective. In a large, shallow tray, the soil is contoured to accommodate all eleven trees in relation to each other, with the largest tree, A, at the front of the centre line to the right. Put B to the left, further towards the rear.

Step 6

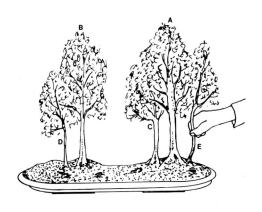

Now position the rest of the trees, in descending order of size, always relating them to their predecessors. Tree C, therefore, will be allied to A, that is a little to the left and the rear of the largest tree. Tree D will be placed in a similar position to the second largest tree B, and so on. Continue potting in this way until the smallest tree is finally closest to the back of the pot, representing the most distant tree to be seen in the forest.

simple and relaxing because most have their favourite wood from which to draw inspiration. Depending on the scene being recreated, most trees are suitable for groups. It is possible to mix species, but this is more difficult, especially when flowering and fruiting trees are used which do not mix well with others.

Specific plantings to give a copse or spinney effect, as in the first part of this project, need only a few trees, always an uneven number, if there are less than ten, and common evergreens such as pine, juniper and cryptomeria are popular. Maple, larch and zelkova elms are also much used in small groups. For a larger woodland scene, most deciduous species, like ash, beech, birch and hornbeam are excellent, although oak should be avoided. Remember that the bare shape of the trees in winter should equal the attraction of summer foliage. Beech, of course, hold their leaves in winter and have lovely grey trunks, as do ash.

Trees growing in forest-like profusion of twenty upwards are usually deciduous saplings with little or no intrinsic merit, but creating a memorable effect of depth and density when planted together. Even with such large numbers, accurate placement is important. Technically you should be able to see every tree from the front as well as from either side. Young trees, planted *en masse* by the handful in this way are sometimes referred to by the Japanese term of 'fist planting'. It is easier to achieve a good effect if the trunks are all fairly upright, but otherwise there are few inhibiting factors governing such grouping.

As discussed in relation to raft bonsai, group plantings should not be confused with other multi-trunk styles. When looking at group copses and spinneys, it is easy to mistake them for the Japanese style of clump planting in which single trees throw out several suckers which then are cultivated as individual trunks. However, the most commonly found trees for clump styles are maple, quince and yew which are not usually employed for groups.

Group plantings should reflect the growth habits of wild trees, surrounded by other forest trees, as they struggle towards the light. Obviously growth varies, due to the amount of light received, according to each tree's position in relation to its neighbours. Individual trees not overshadowed will have more abundant branches and foliage, and different parts of the same woodland will be at varying stages of growth depending on light intensity. For this reason, the overall shape of a group must never form an equilateral triangle, but should always have one relatively steep, short side and one long, sloping side (see Step 4).

This is a further reason why classically shaped individual bonsai, with well-spaced branches growing out evenly from the trunk on either side, are inappropriate for groups. Trees that are preferred for groups have long straight trunks, and the more trunks there are in a group the less branches will be needed. You should therefore look for trees with predominantly one-sided branching, particularly full outer branches and scanty inside ones.

Only seedlings and rooted cuttings can be successfully transplanted into groups without any prior training. All wild trees and most established nursery varieties benefit from being trained for a year or more in as shallow a tray as possible to flatten the rootball. This facilitates positioning and adjustment in relation to other trees when potting, as preconceived ideas change and you think it best to move a tree from its original site.

While waiting for the flat rootball to become established, train only those outer branches which will form the outline of the triangular shape. Never forget, however, that you might change your mind about their position, so do not remove any unwanted branches from the inside at this stage. Only when the tree is finally potted in place should you feel free to trim the branches. Basic rules to remember are that front-pointing branches only need retaining for trees near the front of the group, and back branches should be kept on trees at the rear of the container. Outside branches will, of course, remain at the outer extremities.

It is worth repeating here that in small groups the emphasis is less on the position of each tree than its relationship to the others in the group. Groups are viewed from the front at eye level, but certain attributes of good groups can be seen from the side and above. Never put one tree directly in front of another, and check from the side that the trunks do not cross over each other in an untidy manner. The side trees can lean outwards slightly as they do in the wild, and the whole group should lean slightly forwards.

Group plantings represent either close up or distant views. Generally small groups give the impression of small woods near to the viewer, while larger numbers portray whole forests far away, although these can be reversed. To create a close-up scene, as in the first part of this

The three zelkovas seen on pages 90 and 91 have now been incorporated in this large group on a shallow tray. The large middle tree from the threesome is third from the left in the left-hand group here, and the largest tree in the right-hand group was on the left of the threesome. The impression of a much larger woodland seen from a distance is created by putting the largest tree at the front and working back in descending order of size.

project, the smallest tree must be planted nearest the front of the container. The remaining trees, ascending in size, are placed in varying stages to the side and rear of the first one until the largest tree is positioned close to the back of the pot.

To recreate a more luxuriant, distant woodland, increase the number of trees and reverse the placings so that, in simple terms, the largest tree is nearest the front of the container and the smallest closest to the back. This effect is easier to achieve with many trees, and the bigger the differences in size, the greater the impression of depth. Tall, thin trees are best for this style, the tallest tree possessing the thickest trunk and the smallest tree the thinnest.

For this far-away style plant only the back two-thirds of a large shallow tray. Do not try to rush the basic preparation of the container (Step 2), as it can take hours to ensure that the soil is packed firm and contoured according to the position of the trees. Hold the trees upright when checking their placement, and remember that what might seem a difference of only a few centimetres may make a real change in the overall effect. Work against a plain background so that nothing detracts from the basic shape.

Above: Over thirty trident maple saplings grouped so that the smallest tree is at the front and the tallest is at the rear. This forms an illusion of a dark dense forest apparently very close at hand.

Left: This group of five larch appear to be on the middle ground of a relatively barren area. Again, the sense of distance is created by the largest tree being at the front of the group, to the left. Note how all the trees are planted to the rear of the tray.

With the tallest tree on the highest ground at the front of the group, it appears to be on a hill.

The value of a flat rootball will now be appreciated as it is all too easy for the trees to fall over in such shallow soil. Once potted, however, and sheltered from rough winds, the group should become stabilized in its container within six to eight weeks. During this time, while watching over it and watering as necessary, you will be able to gauge whether or not the planting is successful and what further training is needed. After the group has become established, you can decide whether it is sufficiently strong for it to stand alone, whether other trees should be added to form a larger group, or even whether it is not a success and would be best taken apart so that any of the trees with promise can be grown as individual bonsai.

The beauty of groups is this very flexibility. Equally, the same effect can be achieved with much less effort, by those people with less time, by creating a group planting in a window box. Phisically, this is much easier as you have a greater depth of soil to work with than in a shallow tray, and the visual effect will be very similar when viewed from inside a room.

Project 6
Bonsai Landscapes

Above: The components from which the desert scene opposite will be created. Grouped together on and around a cheap plastic tray are the lichen-covered rocks, and from left to right Opuntia brasiliensis, Crassula lycopodiodes, Mammillaria prolifera, Stapelia variegata and Euphorbia mammillaris.

Left: The finished winter desert with white sand swirling up to the rocks around and out of which the cacti grow.

The Japanese love for encapsulating nature in miniature extends beyond growing individual dwarfed trees to the creation of equally impressive small-scale landscapes. This scaled-down reproduction of stylized natural scenes is not, however, a specialized sideline of bonsai production, but is covered by the two separate arts of bonkei and saikei.

Although both these skills can be generally summed up as the recollection of landscapes, or gardens in miniature, the main difference lies in the approach to the subject matter, as well as the diversity of materials and their uses. In simplistic terms, bonkei are idealized three-dimensional pictures of various aspects of country life throughout the year, created usually on a flat tray but also in less conventional containers, framed or free-standing. Bonkei can be 'live', when they incorporate living plants and frequently feature water as part of the design, or dry, when they are composed solely of artificial matter. Often artificial trees and plants are combined with real ones to achieve varying effects, as are such man-made features as tiny houses, temples and pagodas, bridges and boats and even miniature figures. Successful bonkei demands finesse in use of colour and in moulding keto, a peat-like substance from which mountains and other landscape contours are formed. It is very much a modeller's art, the practitioner being more closely allied to miniaturist painters

Step 1

Always bearing in mind the finished effect, the main static elements of the composition — in this case large rocks — are first put in position. Here they are placed to the back and sides of the shallow tray so that the living material can be grouped around them. To gain a natural effect, make sure that the striations on the rocks are running in the same direction. A layer of coarse drainage sand is scattered over the base of the tray which has been previously drilled to provide drainage holes.

Step 2

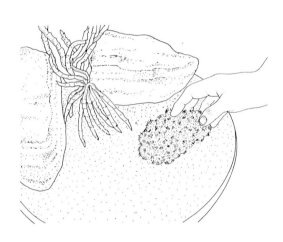

Try to create an impression of wide open spaces by careful placement of the living matter in relation to the rocks. Here, after a layer of cacti soil mix has been put all over the tray, the octopus-like euphorbia is placed in the middle of the rocks, as if growing through them. Find the best position for a clump of dumpy mammillaria, in the foreground as if close to the viewer.

Step 3

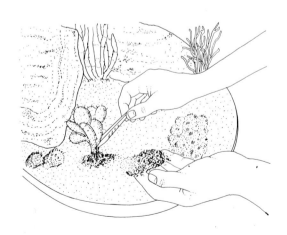

Do not attempt to plant a prickly cactus like this opuntia by hand, as you will be covered in dozens of tiny, painful spines that are difficult to dislodge and may work into the skin. Pick up a cactus at its base with a pair of tweezers and hold it firmly in place as you heap more soil around the roots. This is particularly important with plants, like cacti, which have very short root systems, so must be securely positioned.

Step 4

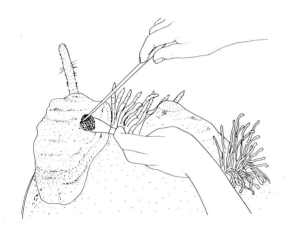

For an even more natural effect, as if the plants are actually growing on the rocks, find a suitable cavity and fill it with soil. If the crevice is shallow, hold a small amount of soil on a spatula close to the hole and firm it in place with a chopstick. A large cactus, in danger of falling over, can be fixed in place with lengths of wire and a metal sinker (Project 3, Steps 3 and 4). The tall, spiky stapelia has been put behind the rocks, as if growing over them.

Step 5

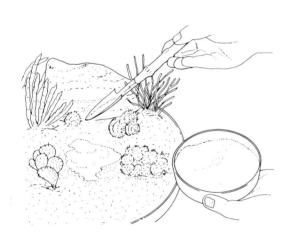

With all the plants in place, complete the scene by sprinkling on coloured sand to represent the overall surface. On top of a layer of yellow sand used as desert background, white sand is added to give an impression of light snowfall. It is put on with a trowel which avoids too much sand falling on top of the cacti. The sand can be built up in large mounds to denote snow drifts, as here, or used to create sand dunes, hills, etc.

Step 6

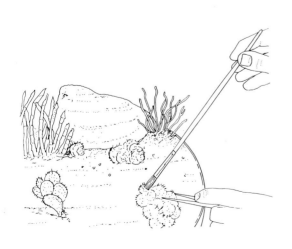

Any excess sand which does spill onto the cacti should be removed, although this may prove difficult as it sticks to the spines and attempts to dust it away can dislodge the precariously rooted plants. The best method is to hold the cactus in place with tweezers, and use a fine hair brush to wipe away any stray sand particles and generally tidy the scene.

The components for constructing the meadow landscape below. Back, left to right: rooted conifer cuttings, potting compost, box tree; front, left to right: coarse sand, jasmine, moss.

and sculptors than to gardeners, although the inspiration is drawn from the highest appreciation of nature.

Saikei, a much younger pursuit, uses only living materials such as seedlings and rooted cuttings, in conjunction with small rocks and stones, to form tiny landscapes. Less formal, with fewer rules than the older arts, it usually appeals to those of a more adventurous and romantic nature.

Both saikei and bonkei are, as noted earlier in relation to group plantings, very different from Western miniature gardens which are generally housed in deep tubs such as half barrels or old sinks. The other major difference is that the plants used are dwarfed strains, bred specially for the purpose, which do not grow beyond a certain size and therefore require little specialized cultivation after the initial scheme has been established. Some European and American miniatures do incorporate occasional features such as tiny stone ornaments, an arch or trellis for climbers or even, if the occasion demands, a small windmill or other building. The main emphasis, however, is usually on the planting and the relationship of the trees, flowers and foliage. To the Western mind, a garden is a garden and that is what is produced in miniature as in actuality.

Just as the more rigid Japanese bonsai styles do not appeal to Western sensibilities, likewise some of the intricately fashioned bonkei and the simple form of saikei are similarly not appreciated. In this section we have, therefore, simply attempted to summarize the main ideas behind Japanese miniatures together with some basic methods of planting and display. Anyone interested in growing bonsai can then, if wished, incorporate the tiny trees into landscapes of their own making, along with other plants and materials.

The path winds into the soft hills and the hedge recedes into the distance in this evocative country scene where the contours of the soil are as important to the overall effect as the individual trees.

The main difference between this tri-part project and the previous one is that in group plantings, whichever trees are used, the end result is virtually always the same kind of scene, despite the varying number of trees, but here the landscapes are never the same. However many bonsai are *grouped* on a shallow tray, and whether they conjure up a copse, spinney or dense woodland, in the end they represent part of a forest. In a tray landscape, however, while a single tree, two or three windswept ones, or even a small coppice might be included, they are but single elements in the total environment. As a lone bonsai aims to recapture one memorable aspect of nature, the miniature 'gardens' attempt to recreate a whole scene. Thus the trees, however attractive in their one right, do not stand alone but complement other equally important features such as water, rock formation or the contours of the earth.

The three landscapes depicted here — a desert under snow, a fertile plain at the foot of rolling hills and a rugged coastal bay — should only be considered as representing an unlimited number of such memorable scenes. They are also personal reconstructions; each would be different in the eye of the beholder. The desert is a recreation of a winter's day in Mexico, where the contrast of the white snow over the yellow sand left an indelible mark on the inner eye of a person accustomed to more temperate climes. The meadow, with its hedge, trees and path leading to the gentle slopes, was based on part of the Sussex downland, but could equally apply to parts of Vermont or the Loire Valley, and the supposed Scottish headland stands for all such wild coast.

It is best, however, to recall a landscape with particular personal associations than to try to produce a 'typical' scene. If your memory fails, there is no harm in consulting a photograph of the place, but do not be side-tracked into including every feature instead of simply bringing back a general mood. As with bonsai, you are not merely creating an exact small replica but an idealized scene in which all the elements harmonize with one another.

The most successful tray landscapes are those with a heightened sense of perspective. A sense of distance is not so vital in a close-up view, but most memorable scenes include a foreground and a distant vista with a focal point somewhere between the two. The size and positioning of the trees and rocks is a major factor here. As with group plantings, larger trees or objects in the

Step 1

Contrary to expectation, a real sense of perspective can be gained in a narrow container. In a tray just 30 × 45 cm (12 × 18in) as here, skilled planting can evoke distances of up to 16 km (10 miles). Place the largest feature in the scene, here the dwarf box tree, near the front of the tray and to one side. Heap up the soil around the base to secure it. Anything smaller, positioned to the rear of this 20 cm (8 in) tree, will look as if it is receding into the near distance.

Step 2

Landscaping the earth to form distant rolling hills is a fundamental factor in the success of this meadow scene. At the back of the tray, add enough soil to the overall layer to raise it above the rim. Use your hands to mould gentle contours in this raised earth and pat the slopes into a smooth surface with the fingers.

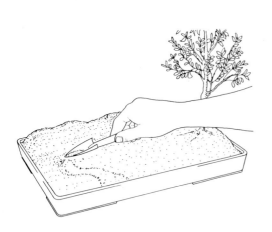

Step 3

Interest is added, and the idea of perspective enhanced, by the addition of a little path which meanders up to the hills. Take a little trowel full of light-coloured sand and sprinkle it in a curving motion from the front edge of the tray to where the 'hills' begin. At the start the path should be about 5 cm (2in) wide, gradually becoming narrower and lighter over a distance of some 10 cm (4in) until it is merely a grain or so thick where it disappears.

Step 4

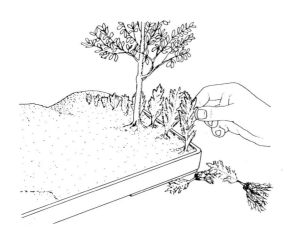

Make a hedge to accompany the large tree from several young rooted cuttings of any appropriate species. You will need relatively large numbers for a thick hedge, in a range of sizes. To reinforce the impression that the hedge too is receding, grade the cuttings or seedlings and plant the largest near the front of the tray, going down in size to the smallest at the rear.

Step 5

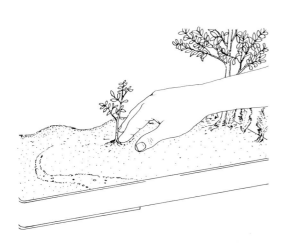

As more elements are added, it will become apparent that others are needed. At this stage the large tree has been balanced by the hedge on one side, but is separated from the path to the extent that the two do not relate. By putting in a smaller tree such as this jasmine, placed behind and to the left of the box tree, a more harmonious composition is achieved, and the sense of perspective heightened.

Step 6

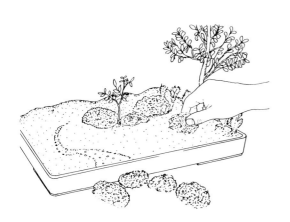

Complete the scene by bringing in different colours and textures. Distribute clumps of moss round the trees to help secure them and to prevent water loss. Lighter green, springy moss for the general surface makes good substitute grass, while darker shades of moss over the contoured slopes add to the 'reality' of the distant hills.

foreground and smaller ones towards the back, give an impression of depth. The same principle applies to features such as paths and streams which start wide and gradually taper off as they supposedly go farther away.

The first essential for this type of garden is the container. Avoid the pretty, more expensive type of tray, perhaps lacquered, as very little can be seen once they are covered with soil. Also, the trays must have adequate drainage holes which should be drilled or punched in, so a colourful, relatively inexpensive plastic or tin tray is perfectly adequate.

The type of soil used, as always should reflect the material growing in it. Obviously a specific cacti mix is used for the desert scene, but a general mixture of sterilized soil and soilless compost is normally acceptable. Clay and peat make a firm base for plants on rocks or in cavities. The art of forming contours with the soil is vital to good tray landscapes, a point where bonkei skills are useful, although here it is the action of the hands and fingers, patting down and

smoothing in place, which is more important than shaping with a tool.

Rocks and stones of varying shapes and sizes are perhaps the next most important component. Look for them at the same time as when searching for suitable homes for rock-clinging bonsai, although the landscape rocks are generally smaller. And, whereas a single rock on which to put a bonsai can have strikingly individual qualities, unless you are seeking a particularly singular peak or cliff face, it is better if the rocks in each garden are similar in colour and texture. To back up the impression of real cliffs, make sure that when the rocks are positioned on the tray, the striations — lines running through them — are all going in the same direction.

Various kinds of sand are an essential part of tray landscapes. Again, do not use sand from the beach, but buy horticultural sand. A coarse variety is frequently mixed with the soil to aid drainage, and others of different colours and consistencies can be used to portray all kinds of surfaces. Much depends on personal taste. While a bright blue type of fish tank gravel may seem ideal for a small stream or pond to one person, it may not appeal to another. Experiment with what is to hand, so long as it cannot harm the living matter. Plain grit from the roads, for example, makes a good basic scree and a few grains of washing powder add a realistic touch of 'white horses' to the tops of curling waves.

Moss is also very useful when creating mini-landscapes. As well as denoting colour variations and different surfaces, it also helps bind the shallow soil together and keeps it moist. You can simply take up moss and press it in position to create an immediate effect, but it may die back before becoming established if the conditions are not right. If you can contain your impatience at wishing to finish off the scene, put small lumps of moss in place on the surface soil, cover with another light layer of soil, firm down and water. The new moss should begin to sprout in about ten days.

If moss is in short supply, make sure of an available source by growing your own. Leave

a lump to dry, then pound it finely in a mortar or pass through a sieve. Add about one third moss to two-thirds soil and put on top of a layer of soil, pressing in place and spraying regularly with water so that it never dries out. The moss will begin to form in a little over two weeks.

Live material used in tray landscapes depends on the scene in question. Cacti, naturally, are used in a desert scene, and a compact variety of heather would be at home on an upland. Once again, do not be too literal in your choice of plants for different situations. The larger tree in our English meadow landscape was a box and the smaller a jasmine, hardly a typical combination but one that *looked* right in context. If you intend to alter the landscape from time to time, or even to renew it entirely, you will naturally be

The bleak coastal bay (below) with waves washing onto a deserted beach where only the rocks stand firm against the powerful winds and the stunted trees bow in submission is formed from such simple objects as rocks, sand, moss and seedlings (facing page), all welded together by artistic skills and the power of the imagination.

Step 1

From a collection of small to medium sized rocks and pebbles, choose three or four of different shapes, but of similar colour and texture, which fit together well. Cover the surface of a plastic or tin tray with a layer of clay and peat mixture. Position the rocks in a natural-looking formation, curving round about two-thirds of the rear of the tray, making sure that the lines on them are all running the same way.

Step 2

Press home any remaining soil mix into the crevices between the rocks. Using varying shades of moss, press clumps in place behind, on top of and at the base of the rocks as appropriate. Powdered moss, if sown correctly, will give an all-over cover within weeks, but the landscape will look rather bare until it starts to grow.

Step 3

Add a living element to the scene by including one or more tiny trees. If you do not want to disturb a bonsai, use rooted cuttings again. The needle juniper shoots being planted here look very like the type of trees to be found in such a wild situation. Plant them at a slight angle, at the side or top of the rocks to make it look as if they are bending in the wind.

Step 4

Form the beach in the foreground by trickling light-coloured sand of varying depths in a semi-circle beneath the rocks. The colour and thickness of the sand can be altered as befits the scene, with perhaps a darker shade round the 'water's edge' and a line of white sand at the foot of the rocks where it might be driest. To complete the picture, a swirling layer of heavier greyish sand round the perimeter represents the sea, with a few grains of washing powder for waves.

reluctant to risk valuable or immature bonsai. When only small trees are needed, it is best to use seedlings or rooted cuttings of various sizes. These may achieve a surprisingly realistic effect, as well as providing a point of interest as they mature. Equally, it is not such a loss if they fail to take.

If a larger tree is required, take the opportunity to include some of your less successful bonsai which do not quite make the grade as individual trees, are too advanced to include in a multi-group planting, and may well take on new meaning in a landscaped setting. As the tree has

to grow in relatively shallow soil on the tray, it is essential that it has already received training in a bonsai container and has a comparatively flat rootball.

You can thus adapt your bonsai skills to a related form of creativity. The beauty of this type of miniature is that a scene can be put together — and even undone if required — within hours. All kinds of containers and settings are permissible, from a window box to the shallow top of a wall. And an indoor arrangement makes an unusual change to greet guests instead of the conventional flowers.

Further Reading

There are far too many gardening books with general advice on tree cultivation to be included here. Similarly, of the available books on bonsai and its allied arts, many are rather esoteric for the general taste, being direct translations from the Japanese. The following titles are to be recommended for their sound basic approach towards all trees and bonsai growing in particular. Several have the advantage of being well illustrated, with colourful examples of bonsai styles and monochrome photographs of essential techniques.

ADAMS, Peter SUCCESSFUL BONSAI GROWING (Ward Lock, London 1978)

HART, C. BRITISH TREES IN COLOUR (Michael Joseph, London 1973)

HILLIER, H. (Ed) HILLIER'S MANUAL OF TREES AND SHRUBS (David & Charles, Newton Abbot 1978)

HIROTA, J. BONKEI: TRAY LANDSCAPES (Phaidon, Oxford; Harper & Row, New York; Kodansha International Ltd, Tokyo 1974)

KAWAMOTO, T. SAIKEI: LIVING LAND-SCAPES IN MINIATURE (Phaidon, Oxford; Harper & Row, New York; Kodansha, Tokyo)

KAWASUMI, M. BONSAI WITH AMERI-CAN TREES (Phaidon, Oxford; Harper & Row, New York; Kodansha, Tokyo 1978)

LARKIN, H. J. BONSAI FOR BEGINNERS (Angus & Robertson, London 1976)

MURATA, K. and K. BONSAI (Hoikusha Publishing, Osaka 1977)

WALKER, Linda M. BONSAI (Gifford, London 1978)

List of Suppliers

General nurseries have been recommended throughout this book as providing many suitable trees to grow as bonsai. Also, many major seedsmen sell bonsai tree seeds, either direct or through general retail outlets, garden centres, etc. There are, however, a number of specialist bonsai nurseries, several of which import trees direct from Japan and which also supply tools and literature.

Bromage & Young Ltd, Wildacre, Brookhurst Road, Cranleigh, Surrey

Glenside Bonsai, 98 Richmond Road, Freemantle, Southampton, Hants

Price & Adams, Cherry Trees, 22 Burnt Hill Road, Wrecclesham, Farnham, Surrey

Sei-yo Kan Bonsai (J.A.S.B. Ltd), 20 Battersea High Street, London SW11

Thompson & Morgan Ltd, London Road, Ipswich, Suffolk

Tokonoma Bonsai, 14 London Road, Shenley, Radlett, Herts

Bonsai Societies

Too many localized bonsai groups exist to list here. However, the main national societies can recommend area, state, or even town associations and local suppliers.

Bonsai Societies in the UK

Bonsai Kai of the Japan Society of London
Hon. Sec. Japan Society of London, 656 Grand Buildings, Trafalgar Square, London WC2

Hon. Sec. Bonsai Kai of the Japan Society of London, 39 West Square, London SE11

British Bonsai Association, 23 Nimrod Road, London SW16

Bonsai Societies in the USA

American Bonsai Society, 953 South Shore Drive, Lake Waukomis, Parkville, Mo. 64151

Bonsai Clubs International, 480 Oxford Street, Arcadia, California 91006

Bonsai Society of Greater New York Inc., Box E, the Bronx, New York, N. York 10466

California Bonsai Society, PO Box 78211, Los Angeles, California 90016

Acknowledgments

The author and publishers would like to express their thanks to Bromage & Young Ltd, Cranleigh, Surrey, and to Anne Swinton for her expert advice and for the loan of many of the trees photographed in this book. They are also grateful to David Parr and Ron Haywood for their work on the line drawings and to the following for permission to reproduce the photographs on pages 10—11, 13 top and bottom, 17 The Smithsonian Institution, Freer Gallery of Art, Washington DC; 12, 32 Hoikusha Publishing Co. Ltd, Osaka; 14—15 The New Otani Hotel, Tokyo; 44 top Murphy Chemicals Ltd, St Albans; 44 middle G.E. Hyde, Doncaster; 44 bottom, 45 (all three) Harry Smith, Chelmsford.

Index